THE IRISH MAIL

Dedicated to the memory of my late wife, Alwen, who offered constant support throughout my writing career. That support is still very sadly missed.

BR 'Britannia' Pacific No. 70031 *Byron* leaves the Penmaen-bach Tunnel with an Up express, 21 July 1962. These engines were the mainstay of 'Irish Mail' services from 1953 until replaced by diesel traction in 1960. Penmaen-bach Tunnel is a curved 718 yd structure and is one of the pair designed by Robert Stephenson to solve the problem of taking the railway through the twin headlands that surround Penmaenmawr. In 1917 the tunnel caved in and only prompt action by four railwaymen prevented a major catastrophe when they managed to stop a westbound express full of soldiers hitting fallen rocks.

Peter Owen

THE IRISH MAIL

THE OLDEST NAMED TRAIN IN THE WORLD

MIKE HITCHES

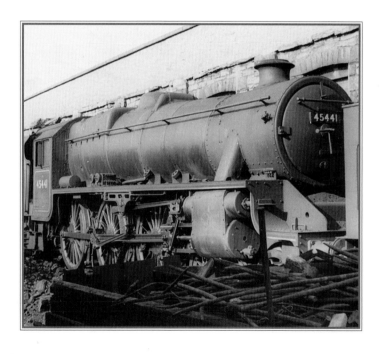

SUTTON PUBLISHING

Sutton Publishing Limited
Phoenix Mill · Thrupp · Stroud
Gloucestershire · GL5 2BU

First published 2000

Title page photograph: An LMS class 5 4–6–0, No. 45441 at Holyhead shed, 29 March 1959. The shed was allocated a number of express engines for use on 'Irish Mail' services, as well as locos for local, freight and shunting work emanating from the port.

Author's collection

British Library Cataloguing in Publication Data
A catalogue record for this book is available from the British Library.

ISBN 0-7509-2301-6

Typeset in 10.5/13.5 Photina.
Typesetting and origination by
Sutton Publishing Limited.
Printed in Great Britain by
Cromwell Press, Trowbridge, Wiltshire.

LMS class 3F 0–6–0T locomotive No. 47410 hauls a long rake of parcel vans and four-wheel goods vans up the incline out of Holyhead, 1964. These little locos worked very hard around Holyhead, often shunting coaches into the station to form the Up 'Irish Mail', where the 'Irish Mail' departs for Ireland.

Norman Kneale

CONTENTS

LMS 'Black 5' No. 5495 heads a Down express through Berkhamsted on the route of the 'Irish Mail' from Euston, 9 October 1948.

R.M. Casserley

INTRODUCTION

While the 'Irish Mail' may not have the romance and glamour associated with other named trains, such as the GWR's 'Cornish Riviera Express', the LNER 'Flying Scotsman' or the LMS 'Royal Scot', it deserves its place in history as the oldest named train in the world, and, as such, the forerunner to all of the others. The train began life in 1848, when it was inaugurated by the LNWR as the service operating from the great London terminus at Euston to the sea-packet port at Holyhead. A railway service, carrying mails to Ireland, had been running since 1839, operated by the London & Birmingham Railway and Grand Junction Railway, to Liverpool and stagecoaches had carried the mails before that for many years. It was, however, the opening of the Chester & Holyhead Railway that allowed rapid transit of mails from London, with Holyhead offering the shortest sea crossing to Ireland. The 'Irish Mail' spawned other named trains operating between Euston and Holyhead, such as the 'The Emerald Isle Express'. Unlike other mail trains, the 'Irish Mail' has always been an express passenger train also carrying mails in order to maximise use of packet boats from Holyhead to Ireland.

The 'Irish Mail' also resulted in improvements to rail services. The train's better times led to the first water troughs being laid anywhere in the world. The 'Irish Mail' was also the train that took Greenwich Mean Time from London to Ireland.

Politics and the 'Irish Question' have been part of the story of the 'Irish Mail' since its inception. The train has provided an important link between Westminster and Dublin over the years and several English and Irish politicians have used the train to try to resolve problems in Ireland. Charles Stewart Parnell, the famous Irish politician, travelled on the 'Irish Mail' frequently in his efforts to gain Irish independence and to sort out problems with his own political party in Dublin. Being the main connection between London and Dublin, the 'Irish Mail' itself has been threatened on numerous occasions by the IRA, who recognised its importance as a communication link between Britain and Ireland. However, no terrorist attacks have ever succeeded in disturbing the running of this train. Despite these problems, the 'Irish Mail' has always been well used, not least in the summer by tourists travelling to and from Ireland for holidays. Also, many passengers have been native Irish people who, due to economic circumstances, live and work in Britain but travel home to visit relatives and families.

The 'Irish Mail' continues to run today under the auspices of Richard Branson's Virgin Railways, over 150 years since its inception and 161 years since a railway connection was established between London and Dublin. However, it no longer transports mail, which is carried by air.

Mails and passengers were travelling between London and Dublin well before 'Irish Mail' trains were even thought of. For centuries Holyhead has been the main departure point for Ireland from Britain, with sailing packets being used for these crossings until 1817, when the first steamers were operated by the New Steam Packet Company. Travel overland from London to Holyhead was usually by private

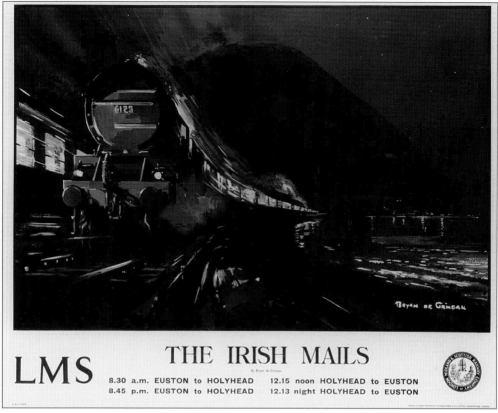

An LMS advertisement for the 'Irish Mail' train service, *c.* 1930. This was also the time when the new 'Royal Scot' 4–6–0 locomotives were introduced on this famous train. These locomotives were to be associated with the 'Irish Mail' for the next thirty years. The location appears to be the town of Penmaenmawr, on the North Wales coast, which was famous for supplying the railway ballast used under the whole of the track over which the 'Irish Mail' ran.

National Railway Museum

coach or horseback until about 1780, when stagecoaches began to operate. Mail coaches, which carried mail as well as passengers, were run between 1812 and 1839, when mail was carried by rail to Liverpool, and from there to Ireland.

In 1710 journeys from London to Dublin could take anything from seven to fourteen days, which was cut to five days when stagecoaches came into use in 1780. The introduction of mail coaches in 1812 further reduced the journey time to four days. The new Holyhead mail coaches, which came into use in 1817, at the same time as steam packets began to operate from Holyhead, meant the journey would only take 55 hours. At the same time, steam packets began calling at Kingstown (later Dun Laoghaire) harbour, which also opened in 1817, instead of Howth, the previous major sea-packet port. By 1826 the journey times had been reduced by another 5 hours, and small improvements continued to be made until 1830 when faster mail coaches were introduced which meant the journey only took 35 hours; this had become 32 hours by 1838.

Not only were journeys slow by today's standards, but they could be rather hazardous. The favoured route for stagecoaches was along the Roman Watling Street,

THE ALLIANCE,

William Roberts, Master, stands I. A.

IS now Loading at Pickle Herring Wharf, London, for Porthdinllaen, Carnarvon, Bangor, Beaumaris, and Amlwch. Apply to the Wharfinger, on the Wharf, or to the Master on board.

THE FOLLOWING

COACHES,

START FORM

MR. SPENCER'S,

EAGLE & CHILD INN,

Holyhead.

The Royal Chester Mail,

Leaves every Afternoon at Two,

Passing though Bangor, Conway, Abergele, St. Asaph and Holywell, and arrives at Chester abouts four o'clock the following morning, in time for the Liverpool and Manchester Mails.

A Light Post Coach, called

The PRINCE REGENT,

Leaves at Nine every Morning,

By way of Capel Curig, through Shrewsbury, Wolverhampton, Birmingham, Coventry, Daventry, Towcester, Stony Stratford, St. Albans, and arrives at the Swan with two Necks, Lad-lane, London, the following morning but one, at half-past seven.

The Royal London Mail,

Leaves every Evening at half-past Four,

By way of Capel Curig, through Shrewsbury, Wolverhampton, Birmingham, Coventry, Daventry, Towcester, Stony Stratford, St. Blbans, and arrives at the Swan with two Necks, Lad-lane, London, the following morning but one, at half-past six.

Performed by the Public's most obedient Servants,

W. JACKSON AND
T. SPENCER & Co.

NEW MAILS,

AND

OTHER COACHES!

Superior and Expeditious Travelling,

FROM

MR. SPENCER'S,

EAGLE & CHILD INN,

Holyhead.

The Royal Chester Mail,

Leaves every Morning at Nine,

Passing through Bangor, Conway, Abergele, St. Asaph and Holywell, and arrives at Chester about eleven o'clock that night, in time for the Mail on to London, through Nantwich, Stafford, Litchfield and Northampton, and arrives in London at six the following morning but one.

A Light Post Coach, called

The PRINCE REGENT,

Leaves at Nine every Morning,

By way of Capel Curig, through Shrewsbury, Wolverhampton, Birmingham, Coventry, Daventry, Towcester, Stony Stratford, St. Albans, and arrives at the Swan with two Necks, Lad-lane, London, the following morning but one, at half-past seven.

The Royal Liverpool Mail,

Leaves at Three every Afternoon,

By way of Capel Curig, through Corwen, Llangollen, Wrexham, and Chester, to Liverpool, where it arrives at half-after six the following morning.

The Royal Manchester Mail,

Leaves every Afternoon at Three.

By way of Bangor, Capel Curig, Corwen, Llangollen, Wrexham, through Chester and Warrington, and arrives at the Swan Inn, Manchester, the following morning, at eleven; where it meets Coaches for Leeds, Halifax, Huddersfield, &c. &c.

The Royal London Mail,

Leaves every Evening at half-past Four,

By way of Capel Curig, through Shrewsbury, Wolverhampton, Birmingham, Coventry, Daventry, Towcester, Stony Stratford, St. Albans, and arrives at the Swan with two Necks, Lad-lane, London, the following morning but one, at half-past six.

Performed by the Public's most obedient Servants,

W. JACKSON AND
T. SPENCER & Co.

An advertisement for stagecoaches operating between Holyhead and London, February 1820. Included is the timing for the 'Royal London Mail', the forerunner of the 'Irish Mail' train, which took 38 hours to reach London.

Author's collection

Mail coaches, operated from the Eagle and Child Inn, Holyhead, advertised in the *North Wales Gazette*, August 1820. Although the coaches were listed as 'New Mails', the journey to London still took 38 hours; the early train journeys reduced this to about 8 hours.

Author's collection

the modern A5 road from London to Holyhead, but there was always the danger of attack by highwaymen, and when coaches became 'non-stop' there was the risk that the driver might fall asleep in the night or a passenger sitting on the top of the coach might literally 'drop-off' to sleep. Anyone who travelled along the coast route, later to be followed by the Chester & Holyhead Railway, had other obstacles to overcome. At Conwy, the river, which has a rapid current, could only be crossed by using the local ferry. Unfortunately, the men who operated these ferries were often drunk and abusive to passengers, and they would only ferry passengers when it suited them and would often leave them in situations where they would have to wade through the waters of the river from the ferry boat to the opposite shore. Having successfully travelled across the river at Conwy, those travelling along the North Wales coast would have to negotiate the twin headlands that surround the modern town of Penmaenmawr. While the eastern headland at Penmaen-bach presented not too many problems, the western headland, Penmaenmawr mountain itself, was very dangerous and the road there was subject to frequent collapse and travellers were known to fall on to rocks below and be lost in the sea. The author Daniel Defoe remarked that this headland was dangerous and he feared for his own life when he once made the crossing. The perilous nature of the route was eased somewhat when Thomas Telford built his coastal Holyhead Road in 1825/6, and evidence of this road can still be seen at Penmaen-bach and Penmaenmawr. He also constructed suspension bridges at Conwy, which put the rude ferrymen out of business, and over the Menai Strait.

In 1820 mail coaches left Holyhead from the Eagle and Child Inn (later taken over by the LNWR as the railway station at Holyhead was developed) at 4.30 p.m. and took Watling Street to arrive at the Swan with Two Necks Inn, Lad Lane, London, at 6.30 a.m. on 'the following morning but one'. Such were the dangers of stagecoach travel in those days that operators always added the caveat 'if God wills' in their advertisements. It was a stagecoach accident along Watling Street that speeded up the demise of this form of travel in favour of railways when, in the early 1830s, an Irish Cabinet Minister was involved in such an incident while travelling from Parliament to his home in Ireland. Following his complaints, investigations were made into the possibilities of establishing railways in North Wales for Irish traffic, which eventually led to the opening of the Chester & Holyhead Railway.

Journeys could be expensive as well as slow, as can be illustrated by the example of one John Russell who, in 1806, decided to travel from London to Dublin in order to stay with his parents for the school holidays. The coach journey to Holyhead took three days, he then crossed the Irish Sea by sailing packet to Ireland, where he took a post chaise, a fast light coach, to Dublin. On arrival, he presented his father with a bill for £31 16s, the total cost of the trip.

The opening of the Stockton & Darlington Railway on 27 September 1825 spelled the end for the stagecoach, although the true potential of rail transport did not become apparent until the opening of the Liverpool & Manchester Railway (L&M) on 15 September 1830. This railway was built as a passenger railway to link these two major cities. The significance of the opening of this line was that it used steam locomotives throughout, and quickly made profits for its investors. Indeed, by the end of 1830 there was a net profit of £14,432 – railway traction had proved its worth. Mail was first carried by rail on 11 November 1830 via the L&M, and within the next few years the Postmaster General made a number of contracts with the railway company for carriage of the Royal Mail. The full benefits of carriage of mail by the railways were not apparent until there was a continuous rail connection between London, Birmingham, Manchester and Liverpool. This was achieved when the Grand Junction Railway (GJR), which ran between Birmingham and the L&M, was opened in 1837 and the London & Birmingham Railway (L&B) opened in 1838. Sorting of mail en route in order to save time was first suggested in stagecoach days, and the Grand Junction Railway put the idea into practice on 6 January 1838, between Birmingham and Liverpool, after they had kitted out a horsebox as a sorting carriage. Having satisfied themselves that the experiment was a success, the GJR built a special vehicle that was fitted with apparatus for picking up and dropping mail at speed. This idea was devised by John Ramsay of the Missing Letters Branch at the Post Office. By February 1839 the new vehicle was reported by the Post Office as being 'perfectly efficient' and came into regular use.

Meanwhile, the directors of the London & Birmingham Railway were trying to obtain mail contracts for themselves and, as a first step, they asked Robert Stephenson to investigate the feasibility of carrying mail by night. Once he had

To solve the problems of crossing the River Conwy and the Menai Strait, Robert Stephenson constructed tubular bridges, the one at Conwy being the model for the much bigger structure that was to cross the Menai Strait into Anglesey. Here, the bridge at Conwy is seen under construction and one of the tubes is being floated out on the river before being jacked up into position. The bridge portals were designed to blend in with the nearby castle, which can be seen on the left. Under the eye of local observers, construction is almost complete, ready for the line to Bangor to open in 1848.

Author's collection

reported back that the railway would be ready for such a service, the directors suggested on 20 February 1838 that 5s 6d per mile, each way, should be charged to the Post Office for the conveyance of mail. The Post Office must have been satisfied because, according to the minutes of the board meeting, a contract between the General Post Office and L&B 'for the conveyance of mails', dated 19 May 1838, was presented to the board on 13 May 1838 and the Company Seal was duly affixed.

During the latter half of 1838 the L&B and GJR began to collaborate in an effort to offer passengers good through services between London, Birmingham, and Liverpool. On 13 July 1838 reciprocal agreements were made to provide through trains via Birmingham to London over L&B metals and, on 13 June 1839, the GJR arranged that their trains were timetabled to accord with through trains of the L&B. Other arrangements were made, including those covering parcels traffic, and this friendly situation was to prove valuable when mail traffic was underway.

Having shown the success of mail trains, mails to Ireland were carried for the first time by rail on 24 January 1839, using the L&B from Euston to Birmingham, and then via the GJR and L&M to the Admiralty Steam Packet Port at Liverpool. Here the mails were transferred to the City of Dublin Steam Packet Company for the sea crossing to Ireland. In this way, mail posted in London in the afternoon was shipped from Liverpool at 7 a.m. the following morning and arrived at Kingstown some 10 or 11 hours later, a total journey time of about 22½ hours. Holyhead was left to deal with local mails and mail from Chester. This situation was, however, only short-lived.

In 1836 commissioners were appointed to investigate the railway system in Ireland. Charles Vignoles was the engineer and in March 1837 he was asked to report on plans made in mainland Britain for connecting railways in England and Wales. If Vignoles had his way then Holyhead and the North Wales coast would not have been chosen for a railway to connect Britain with Ireland. He favoured a route through Mid Wales to a new port at Porth Dinllaen, near Caernarfon. He rejected a route from Chester to Holyhead because he thought the engineering difficulties associated with crossing the River Conwy, Menai Strait and the problems of going around the headlands at Penmaen-bach and Penmaenmawr would be too great. Another alternative was offered by the St George's Harbour & Railway Company, who envisaged bringing a railway along the North Wales coast to Ormes Bay (later Llandudno), but this suggestion was quickly rejected, on the grounds that it was felt that passengers would rather travel direct from Liverpool to Ireland than go overland to Ormes Bay. Holyhead did, however, have the advantage of being an existing steam-packet port, offering the shortest sea crossing to Ireland. It was this, and the fact that Chester was becoming an important railway junction, that influenced the final decision of the authorities to build a line connecting these two points. Engineering difficulties were solved by the great railway engineer Robert Stephenson. He built tubular bridges over the Conwy and Menai Strait and tunnelled through Penmaen-bach and Penmaenmawr. Royal Assent was given for the Chester & Holyhead Railway Bill in 1844, and work commenced, appropriately, on St David's Day, 1 March 1845.

Meanwhile, Captain Mark Huish, Secretary of the GJR, was in dispute with the L&B over that company's dealings with the Manchester & Birmingham Railway (M&B), which threatened to deprive the GJR of much of its traffic. Furthermore, the L&B was also interested in the new Trent Valley Railway, which had a route that

One of the tubes for the Britannia Bridge is being constructed on land before being floated out into the Menai Strait. From there it was jacked up into position and riveted to the next tubular section, which was watched by large crowds. It is said that one enterprising gentleman actually went round the crowd and charged them a penny apiece to witness the process. The tubes were timber-lined and it was this timber that was ultimately to destroy the iron tubes when, on 23 May 1970, the bridge was consumed by fire after boys lit a paper torch while, as they said, they were looking for birds' eggs near the bridge. The replacement bridge is now a single-track cantilever structure, without tubes, and a road deck above to carry the new A55 expressway into Anglesey.

Author's collection

avoided Birmingham altogether. Alarmed at this situation, Huish proposed to mix the gauge of the GJR, which was used by the GWR, arguing that a railway monopoly would be prevented. Startled by this, the L&B called for meetings and, in 1846, the L&B, GJR and M&B amalgamated to form the mighty London & North Western Railway (LNWR), with Huish as General Manager. At about the same time the GWR were preparing to make a bid for Irish mail traffic, using their harbour at New Milford, Pembrokeshire. In order to prevent this the LNWR applied pressure on the Chester & Holyhead Railway Company (CHR) to complete their line and stop the GWR winning the mail contract. In the event the CHR was opened on 1 May 1848, although the Britannia Bridge, which would provide the railway link between the mainland and the Island of Anglesey, did not come into use until 5 March 1850. The opening of the CHR did, however, thwart the ambitions of the GWR.

This book relates the story of the 'Irish Mail' from the days of the stagecoach, through the first railway connection at Liverpool, to its best known route from Euston to Holyhead. The story would, however, be incomplete without detailing the sea crossing and the railway connection between the Irish seaport Dun Laoghaire and Dublin.

CHAPTER ONE

THE 'IRISH MAIL'

*n artist's impression of Conway station just after the CHR opened in 1848, with a passenger train, probably the 'Irish
Mail', approaching from Chester. When the first 'Irish Mail' train arrived at Holyhead the station was very primitive indeed.
 temporary station was authorised in March 1848 at a cost of £800 only because major works were ongoing to develop
nd improve the port at Holyhead. Passengers for Ireland were transported through the town by horsebus belonging to the
oberts' company to Admiralty Pier where they boarded steam packets belonging to the Admiralty. From 1850 mails were
rried by the City of Dublin Steam Packet Company (CDSPC) when the Admiralty ceased to be responsible for the carriage
f mails across the Irish Sea. The LNWR did not obtain the mail contract simply because they did not think they had to bid
r it – as the company ran the train service it felt that it should have the right to send the mails by sea. Following this
ilure the LNWR tried for many years to win the mail contract from the CDSPC. This meant that 'Irish Mail' passengers
id to go on to Admiralty Pier to use CDSPC boats, while other steamer passengers using LNWR boats enjoyed all the
cilities at the improving Holyhead station. Indeed, the CDSPC was able to hold on to the mail contract until 1920, mainly
r political reasons.*

Author's collection

With the opening of the CHR the rail link between London and Holyhead was complete and, as if to celebrate victory over the GWR, the LNWR inaugurated the 'Irish Mail' train on 1 August 1848 when it left Euston at 8.45 p.m. The train worked to Chester where it was handed over to the CHR. As the Britannia Bridge was still not complete at the time, passengers and mails went by coach from Bangor, the mainland terminus of the railway, across the suspension bridge over the Menai Strait and joined another train at Llanfairpwllgwyngyllgogerychrhwndrobyllllantrysiliogogogoch (Llanfair PG), the first station on Anglesey, to continue the journey to Holyhead. This section of the CHR was only opened on the same day as the inaugural 'Irish Mail' started from Euston. The 85 miles from Chester to Holyhead took 3 hours 20 minutes, the train arriving in Holyhead at 7.05 a.m. At Holyhead the Admiralty took charge of the mailbags and they arrived at Kingstown pier at 11.30 a.m., a total journey time of some 15¼ hours from London. When the Britannia Bridge finally opened, the journey time was reduced by an hour.

As a 'prestige' train, the 'Irish Mail' has been in the hands of top-link locomotives since its inception. In 1848 LNWR 2–2–2 locos, known as 'Jenny Linds', a variant of a design by E.B. Wilson and Co. of Leeds, took the train from Euston to Chester. These engines were replaced in 1851 by McConnell-designed 'Bloomer' 2–2–2s. McConnell was the Chief Locomotive Engineer at Wolverton and the engines were nicknamed 'Bloomers' because the driving wheels were exposed in the same way that women's clothes were changing and becoming more revealing. At the opening of the CHR motive power was supplied by the LNWR in the shape of the Crewe 2–2–2 type, along with a 7 ft 2–2–2 No. 187 *Velocipede*, and Crampton rear-drive 7 ft 2–2–2 No. 176 *Courier* for use on 'Irish Mail' services. Complaints of insufficient motive power on the CHR forced the LNWR to send replacements in the form of 7 ft 2–2–2 No. 290 *Rocket*, built at Crewe in 1852, and a new 'Velocipede', both based at Chester. Locomotives No. 18 *Cerberus*, built in July 1857, and *Pegasus* were based at Holyhead. All four engines were specifically sent to the CHR for use on 'Irish Mail' trains.

The CHR was absorbed into the LNWR empire on 1 January 1859 and Crewe began to provide all the locomotives for the 'Irish Mail', their 'blackberry' black liveries becoming a familiar sight on the mail train until replaced by the crimson lake livery of the London Midland & Scottish Railway (LMS) in 1923. Express locomotive livery changed to brunswick green after nationalisation in 1948, and to blue when steam was replaced by electric and diesel power, although diesel locomotives remained green for a few years after this modernisation. Coaches were painted in LNWR plum and spilt milk after the CHR came under the control of the LNWR, becoming crimson lake after absorption into the LMS. In BR days coaches were at first crimson and cream, then, from about 1956, crimson lake, and finally changing to blue and grey in 1965 after modernisation. Today the Intercity 125 sets that operate the 'Irish Mail' train are in the Virgin Railways livery – red and black with white bands.

The Britannia Bridge over the Menai Strait was finally opened on 5 March 1850, completing the through route from Euston to Holyhead. An engraving of the new bridge, a favourite location for later photographers, is seen here shortly after it was opened with early 'Irish Mail' trains on the tracks. Unfortunately, the artist has the track curve going in the wrong direction. From both sides the curve should be to the right and not the left, as later views will show. Along with the 8.45 p.m. 'Irish Mail' from Euston, there was a second 'Mail' which left Euston at 5 p.m., the mails arriving in Kingstown at about 6 a.m. the following morning. Later acceleration of the service allowed this train to leave Euston in the morning. Up 'Mail' trains left Holyhead at 2 a.m., arriving at Euston at 11 a.m., and 7 p.m., this second train arriving Euston at 4.50 a.m. Packet boats left Kingstown at 7.30 a.m. and 1 p.m. respectively. All 'Irish Mail' trains carried both first- and second-class passengers, and

third-class passengers were carried on the 'Irish Mail' from 1 May 1897. Down Sunday 'Mails' left Euston at 8.45 p.m., arriving at Holyhead at 5.49 a.m., and Kingstown at 11 a.m. on Monday morning. Another Down 'Irish Mail' ran from Chester only at 9.55 p.m., connecting with a train from Liverpool, rather than running from Euston, the mails from this train arriving in Kingstown at 6 a.m. Up Sunday 'Mails' left Holyhead at 2 a.m. and 7 p.m., packet boats leaving Kingstown at 7.30 a.m. and 1 p.m. Third-class carriages were attached to these trains.

Jim Roberts

The CHR was absorbed into the LNWR in 1859 and, two years later, a most successful class of 2–2–2, the Ramsbottom-designed 'Problem' or 'Lady of the Lake' class, with 7 ft 6 in driving wheels, was introduced for 'Irish Mail' services between Stafford and Holyhead. These small locomotives had control of these trains well into the 1880s, although they were often double-headed as loads increased. An unknown member of the class can be seen here at the Britannia Bridge double-heading another locomotive as it heads the Up 'Irish Mail'. Note the track curves to the right and not the left as the drawing above shows. By 1852 the fare from Euston to Holyhead was 33s for a first-class ticket, and 24s second class.

Jim Roberts

From its inception, in 1848, the 'Irish Mail' took Greenwich Mean Time from Euston to Holyhead. On arrival at Holyhead the watch was handed to the master of the Kingstown boat, which carried it to Dublin. On return the watch was handed back to the Greenwich messenger at Euston. The watch, carried in a leather case, was delivered daily by Admiralty messenger to the guard of the Down 'Irish Mail' and it was returned by the Up 'Mail'. Throughout the journey the train's arrivals and departures were strictly observed according to the watch and, in the early days, all local station clocks were set to GMT. Here, the watch is being handed to the 'Irish Mail' guard at Euston by the Admiralty messenger, who will call at Euston to collect it on return for resetting for the following day. The practice was continued for ninety-one years and only ceased with the outbreak of the Second World War in 1939. The scene was re-enacted when the 150th anniversary train ran in 1998.

Jim Roberts

A 'Lady of the Lake' 2-2-2 locomotive, No. 28 *Prometheus*, waits with the 'Irish Mail' at Crewe, *c.* 1900. Between Chester and Holyhead the 'Irish Mail' called at Flint, Holywell, Rhyl, Conway, Bangor and Llanfair PG in order to transfer mail bags. By 1854 mail pick-up apparatus had been installed on the CHR and this enabled the 'Mail' to pass some of these stations without stopping, which made the service faster. By 1858 8.45 p.m. 'Mail' trains were arriving at Holyhead by 4.31 a.m., with mails arriving in Dublin by 10 a.m. This allowed Irish merchants to send a reply via the auxiliary 'Irish Mail' at 1.30 p.m. for arrival in London the following morning.

Roger Carpenter collection

A portrait of 'Lady of the Lake' class locomotive No. 279 *Stephenson*, at Stafford, *c.* 1900. These small engines were running the 'Irish Mail' at an average speed of some 42 mph by 1860. By this time the train was having to cover the 263½ miles between Euston and Holyhead at such speeds to maintain timekeeping. In view of this in October 1860 water troughs were laid on the Down line at Mochdre, a mile and a quarter east of Llandudno Junction, which allowed non-stop water pick-up. Water was taken from Mochdre stream under an agreement with Lord Mostyn, who owned a great deal of land in and around Llandudno. These troughs were so successful that they were also laid on the Up line. They were invented by John Ramsbottom, then Locomotive Superintendent of the LNWR, and were the first water troughs anywhere in the world. The Mochdre troughs worked well until problems of water supply from nearby railway reservoirs forced them to be moved to Aber, between Llanfairfechan and Bangor, in 1871. Further water troughs were brought into use at Prestatyn in the 1880s and between Connah's Quay and Flint a decade later.

Roger Carpenter collection

Another 'Lady of the Lake' locomotive, No. 33 *Erubus*, pilots a 'Jubilee' class 4–4–0 on the Down 'Irish Mail' at Stowe Tunnel in the early 1900s.

Roger Carpenter collection

Opposite: A CHR timetable for summer 1852. At that time the LNWR did not have full control over the line from Chester to Holyhead, although the company did supply locomotives for the 'Irish Mail' service. Details of boat connecting with the 'Irish Mail' train are detailed, and the CDSPC steam packet fares; it is noted that 'City of Dublin Co.'s steam packets run in connection with the Mail Trains'.

Author's collection

Visitors are allowed to inspect the Britannia Tubular Bridge, under the guidance of a Servant of the Company.

The Line from Bangor to Carnarvon is now Open for Passenger Traffic.

The Doors of the Booking Offices at all Stations will be closed punctually at the time fixed for departure of the Trains; any person arriving after closing will not be admitted.

Passengers are not allowed to enter the Carriages without Tickets.

CHESTER AND HOLYHEAD RAILWAY.

TIME AND FARE TABLE,

ON AND AFTER THE FIRST OF JULY, 1852.

NOTE.—The Arrival time denotes when the Trains *may be expected*, but Passengers, to ensure being booked, should be at the PRINCIPAL STATIONS **five minutes** earlier, and at the INTERMEDIATE STATIONS **ten minutes** earlier. Passengers at Road-side Stations *are* booked conditionally, that is, on there being room in the respective Classes of Carriages in the Trains. Carriages intended to receive Passengers who are expected by the Trains at the Terminal Stations, should be on the Arrival Side of such Stations five minutes, at least, before the time specified in the Tables. Passengers cannot be re-booked at the Road-side Stations by the Train in which they are travelling. The Times shown in this Bill are those at which the Trains are intended to arrive at the various Stations; but the Company cannot guarantee these Times being kept under all circumstances, nor do they hold themselves responsible for delay.

GREENWICH TIME.

UP TRAINS.

Distance from Holyhead (Miles)	STATIONS.	Morning No. 1	2	3	4	5	6	7	8	9	On Sundays 1	2	3	4
	Classes of Trains on Chester and Holyhead Railway	Mail. 1st & 2nd.	1 & 2. 4th Class attached at Mostyn	1st & 2nd.	1st, 2nd & Parl.	1st & 2nd.	Exp. 1st & 2nd.	1st, 2nd & 3rd.	1st, 2nd & 3rd.	Mail. 1st & 2nd.	Mail. 1st & 2nd.	Parl. 1 & 2.	1st, 2nd & 3rd.	Mail. 1st & 2nd.
	KINGSTOWN	P. M. 7 30	Passengers by this Train from other stations are not allowed to re-book 4th Class at Mostyn.	... [	Dublin	A. M.	9 0	P. M. ...	Time.	P. M. 1 0	P. M. 7 50	...	...	P. M. 1 0
	Leave HOLYHEAD	A. M. 2 0		A. M. 1st and 2nd Class only from Bangor.	A. M. 8 0	...	P. M. 2 30	1 30	P. M. 5 0	7 0	A. M. 2 0	A. M. ...	P. M. ...	7 0
	Arrive at							1 38						
3½	Valley	...			8 8	...	...	1 54	5 8	...	...	...	...	...
9	Ty Croes	...			8 21	...	...	2 4	5 22	...	...	...	...	...
12	Bodorgan	...			8 29	...	...	2 18	5 30	...	...	...	...	...
18	Gaerwen	...			8 42	...	...	2 26	5 44	...	...	...	...	...
21	Llanfair	...		...	[illegible]	[illegible]	...	2 32	5 52	7 30	...	...	...	7 30
22½	Britannia B'dge	...		...	8 54	...	...	9 40	5 58	...	...	...	...	...
25	BANGOR	2 45	A. M. 6 15	9 5	9 30	11 0	3 15	3 30	6 15	7 45	2 45	6 15	5 45	7 45
30½	Aber	* ...	6 28	9 18	9 44	11 13	...	3 43	6 28	...	...	6 29	5 59	...
34½	Penmaenmaur	...	6 40	...	9 56	11 25	...	3 55	6 40	...	...	6 41	6 11	...
39½	CONWAY	3 12	6 55	9 40	10 10	11 40	3 45	4 8	6 55	8 12	3 12	6 55	6 25	8 12
44½	Colwyn	...	7 5	9 50	10 24	11 50	...	4 18	7 5	...	...	7 9	6 39	...
50½	Abergele	...	7 21	10 6	10 41	12 6	...	4 34	7 21	...	...	7 26	6 56	...
54½	RHYL	3 44	7 31	10 16	10 54	12 16	4 15	4 44	7 31	8 40	3 44	7 39	7 9	8 40
58½	Prestatyn	...	7 40	10 25	11 4	12 25	...	4 53	7 40	...	...	7 49	7 19	...
64½	Mostyn	...	7 55	10 40	11 21	12 40	...	5 8	7 55	...	...	8 6	7 36	...
67¾	HOLYWELL	4 8	8 3	10 48	11 29	12 48	4 43	5 16	8 3	9 5	4 8	8 14	7 44	9 5
70	Bagillt	...	8 13	...	11 35	12 54	...	5 22	8 13	...	...	8 20	7 50	...
72	Flint	...	8 23	10 58	11 40	1 6	...	5 27	8 23	9 15	...	8 25	7 55	9 15
77½	Queen's Ferry	...	8 36	11 11	11 55	1 13	...	5 40	8 36	...	...	8 40	8 10	...
85	CHESTER	4 40	8 55	11 30	12 16	1 30	5 10	6 0	8 55	9 40	4 40	9 0	8 30	9 40
126½	SHR'SBURY, le. fr	7 20	8 55	1 40	1 40	1 40	6 50	6 50			...	10 35		
	„ ar. at	9 35	10 40	3 40	3 40	3 40	9 0	9 0			...	12 45		
100¼	L'POOL—lea. for	4 50	9 0	12 30	12 30	3 0	5 45	7 0	9 0	10 30	4 50	9 30	9 0	...
	„ ar. at	5 55	9 50	1 35	1 35	4 5	6 35	8 5	10 5	...	5 55	10 35	10 5	...
136½	M'CHESTER, le. fr	7 30	9 45	11 40	1 40	1 40	...	...	...	...	...	...	...	...
	„ ar. at	10 10	12 5	2 10	4 40	4 40	...	...	...	...	...	...	...	...
122½	M'CHESTER, le. fr	4 50	9 0	11 45	...	...	6 5	6 5	...	...	...	...	...	...
	Via Warrington ar. at	6 15	10 35	1 20	...	...	7 40	7 40	...	...	...	...	...	...
159¼	BIRM'HAM—le. fr	4.45 7.30	9 45	11 40	1 40	1 40	5 25	...	9 50	9 50	4 45	...	...	9 50
	„ ar. at	7.50 1.35	1 10	3 30	5 20	5 20	8 10	...	1 12	1 12	7 50	...	...	1 12
263	LONDON—le. for	4.45 7.30	9 45	11 40	1 40	1 40	5†25	...	9 50	9 50	4 45	...	...	9 50
	„ ar. at	11. 0 6.15	4 0	6 30	9 40	9 40	11 15	...	4 50	4 50	11 0	...	...	4 50

Fares from Holyhead.

STATIONS.	Mail and Express 1 Cl. s. d.	Mail and Express 2 Cl. s. d.	Ordinary Trains 1 Cl. s. d.	Ordinary Trains 2 Cl. s. d.	Ordinary Trains 3 Cl. s. d.	Parl. 3rd. s. d.	Horses 1 s. d.	Horses 2 s. d.	Horses 3 s. d.	Carriages Two wheel s. d.	Carriages Four wheel s. d.	Dogs s. d.
HOLYHEAD	...	...	...	...	3d Class in Anglesey	...	...	...	...	...	...	...
Valley	...	...	0 6	0 3	0 2	0 3	...	...	...	...	...	0 6
Ty Croes	...	...	1 1	0 9	0 4	0 9	...	...	...	...	...	0 6
Bodorgan	...	...	1 6	1 0	0 6	1 0	5 0	10 0	15 0	...	...	0 6
Gaerwen	...	...	2 3	1 6	0 9	1 6	...	...	...	...	...	0 6
Llanfair	5 0	4 0	2 8	1 9	0 10	1 9	7 0	14 0	21 0	7 0	10 6	1 0
Britannia B'dge	...	...	3 0	1 10	1 0	1 10	...	...	...	...	...	1 0
BANGOR	6 0	4 6	3 3	2 1	1 1	2 1	8 9	16 0	24 0	8 9	12 6	1 0
Aber	...	...	5 6	4 3	3 0	2 6	...	...	...	...	...	1 0
Penmaenmaur	...	...	6 6	5 0	3 6	2 10	...	...	...	...	...	1 6
CONWAY	10 0	7 6	7 6	5 9	4 0	3 3	13 0	26 0	39 0	13 0	19 6	1 6
Colwyn	...	...	8 3	6 3	4 6	3 8	...	...	...	...	...	1 6
Abergele	...	...	9 3	7 3	5 3	4 2	16 6	33 0	49 6	16 6	25 0	1 6
RHYL	13 6	10 0	10 6	7 9	5 6	4 6	18 0	36 0	54 0	18 0	27 0	2 0
Prestatyn	...	...	10 9	8 6	6 0	4 10	...	...	...	...	...	2 0
Mostyn	...	...	12 0	9 3	6 6	5 4	21 6	43 0	64 6	21 6	32 0	2 0
HOLYWELL	17 0	12 6	12 6	9 9	7 0	5 7	22 6	45 0	67 6	22 6	33 6	2 0
Bagillt	...	...	13 0	10 0	7 3	5 10	...	...	...	...	...	2 0
Flint	18 0	13 6	13 6	10 6	7 6	6 0	24 0	48 0	72 0	24 0	36 0	2 0
Queen's Ferry	...	...	14 6	11 3	8 0	6 5	...	...	...	...	...	2 0
CHESTER	21 0	16 0	16 0	12 3	8 9	7 0	28 0	56 0	84 0	28 0	42 0	2 0
SHR'SBURY	...	...	25 0	19 3	12 3	...	41 4	78 7	114 9	49 0	63 0	3 0
L'POOL	...	...	18 6	14 3	10 0	...	33 0	66 0	99 0	34 0	50 0	2 6
M'CHESTER	...	...	22 0	16 9	11 9	...	41 0	82 0	123 0	45 6	59 6	3 0
M'CHESTER via Warrington	...	...	22 0	16 9	11 9	...	41 0	82 0	123 0	45 6	59 6	3 0
BIRM'HAM	...	...	29 0	21 9	15 0	..	47 6	94 0	141 0	53 0	67 0	3 0
LONDON	...	...	49 0	35 9	23 7½	...	73 0	146 0	219 0	90 0	104 0	6 0

4th Class Carriages will be attached to the Trains marked (*). † Second Class Passengers will be conveyed by the Express Trains between Chester and London.

DOWN TRAINS.

Dist. from Chester (Mls.)	STATIONS.	Aft. No. 1	Morning 2	3	4	5	6	7	Aft. 8	9	On Sundays 1	2	3	4
178½	Leave LONDON	Mail. P. M. 8 45	H. M. ...	H. M. ...	H. M. A. M. 6 0	H. M. A. M. [illegible]	H. M. A. M. 9 30	P. M. [illegible]	H. M. A. M. 10 0	H. M. P. M. 5 0	H. M. P. M. 8 45	H. M. ...	H. M. A. M. 10 0	H. M. P. M. ...
	[illegible]	A. M.	...	A. M.			P. M.		P. M.		A. M.		P. M.	
52	M'CHESTER	...	...	...	9 45	9 45	11 35		1 15	4 35	...	...	...	...
38	„ via Warrington	...	...	...	...	...	1 30	1 30	5 20	8 30	...	...	...	...
15¾	LIVERPOOL	...	...	7 45	10 30	12 15	1 45	1 45	5 0	8 45	...	...	1 30	8 45
42	SHR'SBURY	...	...	6 45	8 27	10 45	12 35	12 35	4 0	6 35	...	...	...	6 40
	Classes of Trains on Chester and Holyhead Railway	Mail. 1 & 2	1,2,&3	1st, 2nd & 3rd.	1 & 2	1 & 2	1 & 2 Expr.	1 & 2 Parl.	1,2,&3	Mail. 1 & 2	Mail. 1 & 2	Parl. 1 & 2.	1,2,&3	Mail. 1 & 2
	Leave	A. M.	A. M.	A. M.	A. M. *	P. M.	P. M.	P. M.	P. M.	P. M.	A. M.	A. M.	P. M.	P. M.
—	CHESTER	3 9	...	9 15	11 45	1 50	2 55	3 30	6 50	9 55	3 9	7 0	6 30	9 55
7	Qu. Ferry *ar. at*	...	...	9 31	12 1	2 6	...	4 1	7 6	...	...	7 20	6 48	...
12¼	Flint	3 34	...	9 45	12 12	2 17	...	4 22	7 20	...	3 34	7 36	7 3	...
14¼	Bagillt	...	...	9 51	...	...	...	4 33	7 26	...	...	7 42	7 8	...
16¾	HOLYWELL	3 44	...	9 59	12 20	2 27	3 20	4 45	7 34	10 20	3 44	7 48	7 13	10 20
20	Mostyn	...	...	10 9	12 28	2 35	...	5 3	7 44	...	...	7 58	7 21	...
26¼	Prestatyn	...	...	10 23	12 40	2 48	...	5 31	7 53	...	...	8 16	7 37	...
30	RHYL	4 9	7 30	10 35	12 47	2 55	3 42	5 48	8 10	10 42	4 9	8 28	7 49	10 42
34¼	Abergele	...	7 40	10 45	12 56	3 5	...	6 11	8 20	...	...	8 40	7 59	...
40¼	Colwyn	...	7 58	10 59	1 5	3 17	...	6 39	8 34	...	...	8 58	8 15	...
45¼	CONWAY	4 39	8 16	11 13	1 16	3 27	4 10	7 0	8 48	11 15	4 39	9 13	8 29	11 15
50	Penmaenmaur	...	8 30	11 25	1 29	...	...	7 23	9 0	...	...	[illegible] 27	8 [illegible]	...
54¼	Aber	...	8 42	11 35	1 40	3 48	...	7 40	9 10	...	...	[illegible] 40	8 [illegible]	...
59½	BANGOR	5 4	8 56	11 50	1 55	4 5	4 35	8 0	9 22	11 40	5 4	10 0	9 10	11 40
	„ depart	...	9 0	...	2 3	...	...	8 7	...	...	...	...	...	...
61¼	Britannia B'dge	...	9 7	...	2 8	...	...	8 15	...	...	...	...	...	...
63¼	Llanfair	5 19	9 15	...	2 16	...	...	8 35	...	...	5 19	...	...	..
66¼	Gaerwen	...	9 26	...	2 25	...	...	8 45	...	...	...	...	...	...
72¼	Bodorgan	...	9 41	...	2 43	...	...	9 6	...	...	...	...	...	...
75¼	Ty Croes	...	9 51	...	2 51	...	...	9 21	...	...	...	...	...	...
81	Valley	...	10 5	...	3 3	...	...	9 32	...	A. M.	...	...	...	A. M.
85	HOLYHEAD	5 49	10 15	...	3 13	...	5 15	9 45	...	12 35	5 49	...	...	12 35
	Kingstown abt.	11 0	...	...	...	...	10 0	...	...	6 0	11 0	...	...	6 0

Fares from London and other stations to Chester.

STATIONS.	Passengers 1st Cl. s. d.	2nd Cl. s. d.	3rd Cl. s. d.	Horses 1 s. d.	Horses 2 s. d.	Horses 3 s. d.	Carriages 2-wheel s. d.	Carriages 4-wheel s. d.	Dogs s. d.
LONDON	33 0	24 0	14 10½	45 0	90 0	135 0	62 0	62 0	4
M'CHESTER	6 0	4 6	3 0	13 0	26 0	39 0	17 6	17 6	1 0
„ via Warrington	6 0	4 6	3 0	13 0	26 6	39 0	17 6	17 6	1 0
LIVERPOOL	2 6	2 0	1 3	5 0	10 0	15 0	6 0	8 0	0 6
SHR'SBURY	9 0	7 0	3 6	13 4	22 7	30 9	21 0	21 0	1 0

Fares from Chester.

STATIONS.	Mail and Express 1 Cl. s. d.	Mail and Express 2 Cl. s. d.	Ordinary Trains 1 Cl. s. d.	Ordinary Trains 2 Cl. s. d.	Ordinary Trains 3 Cl. s. d.	Parl. 3 s. d.	Horses 1 s. d.	Horses 2 s. d.	Horses 3 s. d.	Carriages Two-wheel s. d.	Carriages Four-wheel s. d.	Dogs s. d.
Qu. Ferry	...	...	1 3	1 0	0 9	0 7	...	...	...	...	...	0 6
Flint	3 0	2 3	2 3	1 9	1 3	[illegible]	5 0	10 0	15 0	5 0	6 0	0 6
Bagillt	...	...	2 6	2 0	1 6	1 2	...	...	...	...	...	0 6
HOLYWELL	4 0	3 0	3 0	2 3	1 9	1 4	5 6	11 0	16 6	5 6	8 6	0 6
Mostyn	...	...	3 9	2 9	2 0	1 8	6 6	13 0	19 6	6 6	10 0	1 0
Prestatyn	...	...	4 9	3 9	2 9	2 2	...	...	...	...	...	1 0
RHYL	7 6	5 6	5 6	4 3	3 0	2 6	10 0	20 0	30 0	10 0	15 0	1 0
Abergele	...	...	6 3	5 6	3 6	2 10	11 6	23 0	34 6	11 6	17 0	1 6
Colwyn	...	...	7 6	5 9	4 0	3 4	...	...	...	...	...	...
CONWAY	11 0	8 6	8 6	6 6	4 6	3 9	15 0	30 0	45 0	15 0	22 6	1 6
Penmaenmaur	...	...	9 3	7 3	5 3	4 2	...	...	...	...	...	1 6
Aber	...	...	10 0	7 9	5 6	4 6	...	...	...	...	...	2 0
BANGOR	15 0	11 0	11 0	8 6	6 0	4 11	20 0	40 0	60 0	20 0	30 0	2 0
„ depart	...	...	...	...	...	...	...	...	...	...	...	...
Britannia B'dge	...	...	11 6	8 9	6 3	5 1	...	...	...	...	...	2 0
Llanfair	16 0	12 0	12 0	9 3	6 6	5 3	21 0	42 0	63 0	21 0	31 6	2 0
Gaerwen	...	...	12 6	9 9	7 0	5 6	...	...	...	...	...	2 0
Bodorgan	...	...	13 6	10 6	7 6	6 0	24 0	48 0	72 0	24 0	36 0	2 0
Ty Croes	...	...	14 6	11 0	7 9	6 3	...	...	...	...	...	2 0
Valley	...	...	15 0	11 9	8 3	6 9	...	...	...	...	...	2 0
HOLYHEAD	21 0	16 0	16 0	12 3	8 9	7 0	28 0	56 0	84 0	28 0	42 0	2 0
Kingstown	...	...	...	...	...	...	35 0	70 0	105 0	35 0	60 0	3 0

* By No. 4 Down Train between Bangor and Holyhead, and Stations in Anglesea, 3rd Class Passengers will be booked.

The Company's Steam Packets run in connection with the Express Train from Holyhead at 2 30 p.m. arriving in London at 11 p.m.; and with the Express Train from London at 9 30 a.m., arriving at Kingstown about 10 0 p.m. Second Class Passengers are now conveyed by these Trains between Chester, Birmingham, and London, at the same through Fares as by the Mail Trains. Fares by Chester and Holyhead Co.'s Packets between Kingstown and Holyhead, 1st Class 11s., 2nd Class 8s. By City of Dublin Co.'s Boats, 1st Class, 12s.

City of Dublin Co.'s Steam Packets run in connection with the Mail Trains.

Note.—Through Horses and Carriages will be conveyed by the Express Trains.† First and Second Class Carriages will be attached to the Parliamentary Trains. The MAIL TRAINS, No. 1, *Up*, and No. 4, *Down*, (in *Anglesey*) will, on Sundays, have Parliamentary Carriages attached.

SINGLE AND RETURN TICKETS FOR THE THROUGH JOURNEY BETWEEN ENGLAND, SCOTLAND, AND IRELAND, ARE ISSUED AT THE UNDERMENTIONED STATIONS:—

IN ENGLAND, SCOTLAND, AND WALES.

Bangor (N. W.)
Birmingham
Bristol
Burslem
Burton
Carlisle
Carnarvon
Cheltenham
Chester
Conway (N. W.)
Crewe
Derby—Dudley
Edinburgh
Glasgow
Gloucester
Grimsby
Holywell (N. W.)
Huddersfield
Hull
Leamington
Leeds
Lincoln
Liverpool
London
Longton
Macclesfield
Manchester
Oxford
Rhyl (N. W.)
Sheffield
Stafford
Stoke
Walsall
Warrington
Wolverhampton
Worcester

IN IRELAND.

Athlone
Ballinasloe
Belfast
Cork
Dundalk
Galway
Kilkenny
Kingstown (Dublin)
Limerick
Mullingar
Newry

The 'Irish Mail', headed by a 'Lady of the Lake' class 2–2–2 and 'Precedent' class 2–4–0, approaches Penmaen-bach Tunnel from Conwy, early 1900s. On 12 January 1899 the Up 'Irish Mail' had a close escape when the sea wall on the other side of Penmaen-bach Tunnel collapsed during a heavy storm. It washed away the railway and caused a Down goods train to crash into the sea, killing both the driver and fireman. At 10 p.m., three-quarters of an hour before the goods train was lost, sea water washed over the tracks just as the Down 'Irish Mail' was passing and even entered the carriages. Had the sea wall been washed away two hours later then the Up 'Irish Mail' would have been involved in the disaster too, with great loss of life. In the event this latter train was stopped at Penmaenmawr station, and the passengers were transferred by road to Conwy where a train was waiting to take them on to Euston.

Author's collection

The Up 'Irish Mail' passes through Llanfairfechan in the early 1900s, double-headed by a LNWR 'Dreadnought' 2–2–2–0 Compound and a 'Jubilee' 4–4–0 Compound. Improvements were made to the night 'Irish Mail' with the introduction of specially constructed sleeping cars from 1 March 1875; a supplementary fare of 5s was charged for a berth. These six-wheeled vehicles had a compartment for ladies and two interconnecting ones for gentlemen, with lavatory facilities at each end. From the 1880s longer eight-wheeled stock came into use, and these had radial trucks for increased sideplay, which enabled curves to be negotiated more effectively. Radial sleeping cars came into use on the 'Irish Mail' from 1882. While sleeping accommodation was provided for first-class passengers from the early days of the 'Irish Mail', it was not until 1928 that such facilities were made available to other passengers.

Author's collection

Another 'Teutonic' 2–2–2–0 Compound locomotive heads the Down 'Irish Mail' over Bushey troughs, *c.* 1900. It is unclear when the title 'Irish Mail' was first used in public timetables. Initially the train was listed in the timetables as just 'Mail' or 'Express Mail' until 1861 when the LNWR entitled it the 'Fast Irish Mail', and later that year changing it to 'Express Irish Mail'. It would seem that the name 'Irish Mail' was introduced early in 1864. Indeed, this picture is actually entitled the 'Wild Irishman' rather than the 'Irish Mail'.

Jim Roberts

The Down 'Irish Mail' passing through Atherstone station in the period before parts of the TVR line were quadrupled, *c.* 1890. The engine appears to be a 'Precedent' 2–4–0. From its earliest days the 'Irish Mail' service was profitable, and the LNWR reported that receipts for carriage of mail on the CHR totalled £30,200 in 1854. There was, however, some inconvenience to passengers in the early days of the 'Irish Mail' because they had to check their own luggage and watch its transfer from train to packet boat at Holyhead, and again at Kingstown. To overcome this problem the LNWR introduced a system of registration for passengers' luggage in 1869.

Author's collection

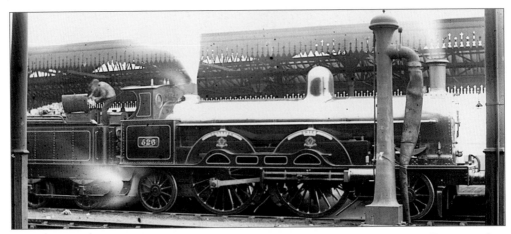

Following the demise of the 'Lady of the Lake' 2–2–2 locomotives on the 'Irish Mail' service other locomotives were seen at the head of this train, including 'Greater Britain' 2–2–2–2 Compounds, introduced by Francis Webb, one of which, LNWR No. 526 *Scottish Chief*, is seen here at Stafford, *c*. 1900. When the 'Irish Mail' service began refreshment facilities were not provided, and there were also complaints about this at Holyhead, although these were resolved by 1850. No refreshments were available for passengers until they arrived at Chester, where there was time for them to use the restaurant there while engines were changed. When the LNWR took sole control in 1859 there was a desire to reduce stopping time at Chester, and in March 1876 luncheon baskets were introduced at Chester on the 'Irish Mail'. Two baskets were offered and contained the following:

Pint of claret or ½ pint of sherry	Pint of ale or stout
Chicken, ham or tongue	Cold meat or pie
Butter, cheese and bread	Cheese and bread
Cost 5s	Cost 2s 6d

This service continued until 1895 when dining saloons were introduced on 'Irish Mail' services. There was a breakfast and luncheon car on the Down 'Irish Mail', which left Euston at 7.15 a.m., and a luncheon and tea car on the Up 'Irish Mail', which left Holyhead at 11.15 a.m.; both had a reputation for good service. Dining cars have been attached to 'Irish Mail' trains ever since, except during the world wars when restrictions were placed on the use of such vehicles.

Roger Carpenter collection

The Up 'Irish Mail' leaves the Britannia Bridge and heads toward Bangor headed by a LNWR 'Precedent' class 2–4–0, *c*. 1900. During the American Civil War the 'Irish Mail' played a part in transmission of news about possible hostilities between Britain and the USA. Britain was sympathetic to the Confederate cause, not least because the southern states provided cotton for Lancashire mills, and the president of the Confederate States sent two envoys to try and gain recognition for the Confederacy. These two envoys were seized by a Federal ship and apologies were sought by the British government, as well as the release of the men. For several days locomotives were kept in steam at Holyhead and a steamer carrying dispatches arrived there at 8.15 a.m. on 7 January 1862. The Queen's messenger collected the mails at Admiralty Pier and the van was pushed to Holyhead station where 'Lady of the Lake' locomotive No. 229 *Watt* was waiting to take the 'Irish Mail' to Euston. The train left Holyhead at 8.28 a.m. and after an engine change at Stafford arrived in Euston at 1.13 p.m., averaging a speed of 54.6 mph. The dispatch contained news of peace, and war with the USA was avoided.

Jim Roberts

Another Up 'Irish Mail' leaves the Britannia Bridge headed by an LNWR 'Experiment' class 4–6–0, late 1900s. From 16 March 1905, following a request from the Post Office, Up 'Irish Mail' trains leaving Holyhead at 12.22 a.m. and noon had an extra van for Liverpool attached, which detached at Chester. The Post Office paid the LNWR an extra *2d* a mile for the service. From 3 July 1905 11½ cwt of mail was carried on the 10.15 'Irish Mail' from Euston to Holyhead and crossed to Ireland on the LNWR express boat to Dublin (North Wall). The Post Office paid the LNWR £650 a year for this facility. 'Irish Mail' timings were accelerated from 1 August 1898 and the Post Office paid the LNWR an additional £6,500 towards the extra costs incurred in speeding up these trains. Under these new schedules the 'Irish Mail' stopped at Rugby, Crewe and Chester only.

Jim Roberts

LNWR 'Prince of Wales' class 4–6–0 No. 1744 heads the Up 'Irish Mail' as it picks up mail from apparatus, 1920. The Post Office attached mailbags to trackside apparatus and these were swept into the train's mail van via a net which was operated just before the train passed. Obviously, this had the great benefit that mails could be collected without the train stopping.

Author's collection

LNWR 'Precursor' class 4–4–0 No. 412 *Marquis* heads the Up 'Irish Mail' at Whitmore troughs, 15 September 1905. Fare dodging has always been a problem on all types of public transport, and it is amazing what lengths people will go to to avoid paying a fare; the 'Irish Mail' was no exception. In the early 1880s a man was found underneath the body of a coach on the Up 'Irish Mail' following its arrival at Chester. He was holding on to a brake rod with his hands and feet, and luckily for him he was unharmed after his journey from Holyhead. The LNWR took legal action against him for travelling without paying his fare and he was fined £1 with the alternative of twenty-one days' hard labour.

National Railway Museum

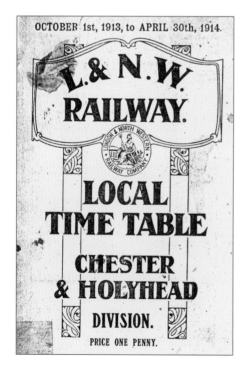

Timetables for the Chester and Holyhead Division, which included the 'Irish Mail' service, from 1 October 1913 to 30 April 1914. By 1896 the LNWR and CDSPC offered an all inclusive fare between Euston and Dublin (Westland Row): 53s 6d single and 93s return for first class; 35s 6d single and 55s 6d return for second class; and 32s 6d single and 51s 6d return third class.

Author's collection

Stn. No.	2 CREWE, CHESTER, NORTH WALES,									
					Week Days.					
		p.m.	p.m.	p.m.	p.m.		a.m.	a.m.	a.m.	a.m.
1	London (Euston) ....depart		8 45	10 15	10 0		12 15			
2	Northampton (Castle) .....,,		9 0	10 23	10 23		1 20			
3	Rugby		10 31	10 55	11 55		2 21			
4	Leicester		9 45	11 15						
5	Leamington		9 0			10Th40				
6	Coventry		10 0				2 43			
7	Birmingham (New Street) ,,		10 15	10 55	10 55		3 15			
8	Stafford		11 1	12 18	1 18		4 16			
9	Leeds (via Stockport)		8 15	10 40	10 40					
10	Manchester (London Rd.)		10 45	12 5	12 5					
11	Crewe ....depart		12 7	1 25	2 5		5 0			
12	Worleston									
13	Calveley									
14	Beeston Castle and Tarporley									
15	Tattenhall Road									
16	Waverton									
17	Chester ....arrive		B		2 32		5 30			
18	Birkenhead (Woodside) ..arrive				3 15		7 5			
19	Preston ....depart	8 15							2 40	
20	Leeds									
21	Manchester (Exchange)...,,	11 15								
22	Warrington		11 57							
23	Liverpool (Lime Street)..depart	11 10		11 55	11 10					
24	Bristol (via Severn Tunnel)depart		7 40				12 37			
25	Shrewsbury		10 50				3 40			
26	Birkenhead (Woodside) ,,	11 20								
27	Chester ....depart	12 20	B	0	2 48		5 50			
28	Sandycroft	0					5 52			
29	Queen's Ferry						6 4			
30	Shotton									
31	Connah's Quay						6 11			
32	Flint				3 5		6 17			
33	Bagillt						6 24			
34	Holywell Junction						6 29			
35	Mostyn						6 37			
36	Talacre						6 44			
37	Prestatyn						6 53			
38	Rhyl { arrive / depart				3 32 / 3 37		7 4 / 7 8			
39	Foryd						7 8			
40	Abergele and Pensarn						7 14			
41	Llandulas						7 23			
42	Llysfaen						7 27			
43	Old Colwyn						7 32			
44	Colwyn Bay			C			7 35			
45	Mochdre and Pabo						7 44			
46	Llandudno Junction ....arrive				4 4		7 55			
47	Llandudno ....arrive			6 50			8 20			
48	Bettws-y-Coed			5 22			9 5			
49	Llandudno Junction ...depart				4 11		8 6			
50	Conway						8 10			
51	Penmaenmawr						8 19			
52	Llanfairfechan						8 25			
53	Aber						8 30			
54	Bangor ....arrive				4 32		8 40			
55	Carnarvon ....arrive				5 10		9 20			
56	Afonwen				6 0		10 20			
57	Bangor ....depart				4 45		8 52	9 12		
58	Menai Bridge						9 16	9 2		
59	Llanfair						9 23	9 8		
60	Gaerwen { arrive / depart				5 0 / 5 3		9 28 / 9 13			
61	Bodorgan						9 18			
62	Ty Croes						9 29			
63	Rhosneigr						9 37			
64	Valley						9 41			
65	Holyhead ....arrive	1 55	2 17	3 30	5 40		9 55 / 10 0			
66	Dublin { Westland Row arr / North Wall ,,	6 0	6 0		7 30					

For Notes to References see page 11.

Timetables for 1913–14 showing Down day and night 'Irish Mail' services.

Author's collection

Stn. No.	AND DUBLIN—continued.				5
			Week Days—continued.		
		a.m.	a.m.	p.m.	p.m.	a.m.
1		7 10	8 30			
2		8 34	9 10			
3		9 4	9 12			
4		8 15				
5		8 15	9 45			
6		8 29	9 37			
7		9 15	9 55			
8		10 36	11 6			
9		8 28	9 28			
10		10 15	10 40			
11		11 17	11 48			
12		11 24				
13		11 31				
14		11 36				
15		11 44				
16						
17		11 55	12 15			
18				1 16		
19			9Sx3s			
20			9 0			
21			10 45			
22			11 31			
23			11 10			
24						11 55
25						
26			11 15			
27			12 23	12 30		12 40
28						12 50
29						12 54
30						12 57
31						1 1
32						1 6
33						1 11
34						1 19
35						1 26
36						1 34
37						1 40
38			1 8	1 22 / 1 30		1 48
39			1 12			1 55
40			1 19			1 59
41						2 5
42						2 12
43						2 16
44			1 29			2 20
45			1 33			2 23
46						2 30
47			1 44			2 53
48						
49			2 2			2X52
50			2 50			
51			1 48			
52			1 52			
53			2 1			
54			2 7			
55			2 13			
56			2 23			
57			2 52			
58			3 52			
59			2 34			
60			2 37			
61			2 43			
62			2 48			
63			2 52			
64			3 3			
65		2 5	3 9 / 3 13 / 3 23 / 3 31			
66		5 30				

For Notes to References see page 11.

Left margin (vertical): *For High-Class Reproductions of Early English Needlework consult the . . Misses LEWIS. 1, STANLEY TERRACE, Holyhead. Magnificent Collection of Designs. Work traced and begun.*

Right margin (vertical): *The L. & N. W. R. collect and convey Luggage in Advance for Tourists. (See page 65.)*

Stn. No.		Week Days	Saturday night	Sunday	Stn. No.	Sundays—continued
1	London (Euston) depart		8 45 10 15 10 0			
2	Northampton (Castle)		9 0 10 23 10 23			
3	Rugby		10 31 10 55 11 55			
4	Leicester		9 45 11 15			
5	Leamington		10 0			
6	Coventry		10 0			
7	Birmingham (New Street)		10 15 10 55 10 55			
8	Stafford		11 0 12 18 1 18			
9	Leeds (via Stockport)		8 15 10 10 10 10			
10	Manchester (London Road)		10 45 12 5 12 5			
11	Crewe depart	10 21	12 7 1 25 2 5			
12	Worleston					
13	Calveley					
14	Beeston Castle and Tarporley					
15	Tattenhall Road					
16	Waverton					
17	Chester arrive	10 49	2 32			
18	Birkenhead (Woodside) arrive		3 15			
19	Preston depart	8 25	2 16			
20	Leeds	7 33				
21	Manchester (Exchange)	9 30	7 40			
22	Warrington	10 18	8 42			
23	Liverpool (Lime Street) depart	9 40	11 55 11 10			
24	Bristol (via Severn Tunnel) depart		7 40			
25	Shrewsbury					
26	Birkenhead (Woodside)	10 0				
27	Chester depart	11 12 11 15	12 30 0 2 48 9 55			
28	Sandycroft					
29	Queen's Ferry					
30	Shotton					
31	Connah's Quay					
32	Flint					
33	Bagillt					
34	Holywell Junction					
35	Mostyn					
36	Talacre					
37	Prestatyn					
38	Rhyl { arrive / depart	11 47 12 30 / 11 50	3 32 11 9 / 3 37			
39	Foryd					
40	Abergele and Pensarn					
41	Llandulas					
42	Llysfaen					
43	Old Colwyn					
44	Colwyn Bay	12 5				
45	Llandudno Junction arrive	12 14	4 4			
46	Llandudno arrive					
47	Bettws-y-Coed		5 14			
48						
49	Llandudno Junction depart	12 17	4 11			
50	Conway					
51	Penmaenmawr					
52	Llanfairfechan					
53	Aber					
54	Bangor	12 37	4 32			
55	Carnarvon arrive		5 10			
56	Afonwen		5 47			
57	Bangor depart	12 40	4 40			
58	Menai Bridge					
59	Llanfair					
60	Gaerwen { arrive / depart					
61	Bodorgan					
62	Ty Croes					
63	Rhosneigr					
64	Valley					
65	Holyhead arrive	1 15	1 53 2 17 3 30 5 40			
66	Dublin { Westland Row... arr / North Wall					

Notes:

: —Via Crewe.

A—Leaves Manchester 4.25 p.m. on Saturdays.

a—Via Wrexham, arrives Chester 4.57 p.m.

B—Calls at Chester at 12.51 a.m. to set down passengers, and to pick up passengers from Warrington and stations beyond.

b—Leaves Leicester 2.42 p.m. on Saturdays.

C—Calls at Colwyn Bay at 5.52 a.m. to set down only.

D—Calls at Waverton when required to set down passengers on notice being given by the passenger to the guard.

E—Calls at Beeston Castle on Mondays and Saturdays.

H—Calls at Beeston Castle when required to set down passengers from London on notice being given by the passenger to the guard.

I—Leaves Leicester 1.40 p.m. on Saturdays.

J—Calls to set down passengers only.

K—Calls at Prestatyn on Saturdays only.

M—Mondays only.

O—Horse boxes and carriage trucks will not be conveyed by these trains.

P—Calls at Mostyn at 5.8 p.m. when required to set down passengers from Liverpool on notice being given by the passenger to the guard.

R—Calls when required to set down passengers from beyond Chester on notice being given by the passenger to the guard.

S—Saturdays only.

Sx—Saturdays excepted.

Th—Thursdays only.

X—Arrives Llandudno 2.58 p.m. on Saturdays.

A 1913–14 timetable showing weekend workings for the 'Irish Mail'.

Author's collectio[n]

Opposite: LNWR 'Claughton' class 4–6–0 locomotive as LMS No. 5994 passes Mochdre and Pabo station, 1920. The LNWR became part of the new London Midland & Scottish Railway following the Grouping of 1923 when following the end of State control of the railways during the First World War, the government decided to reduce the 120 or so railway companies then operating to four groups in preference to nationalising the system, which had been advocated by some. At this time both day and night 'Irish Mail' trains included two Post Office sorting vehicles and picked up mail from lineside apparatus at various points between Euston and Holyhead, as well as making stops at Rugby, Crewe and Chester.

Author's collectio[n]

Another 'Precursor' class 4–4–0 heads the 'Irish Mail' through Bushey troughs, picking up water on the way, late 1900s. The 'Irish Mail' has not been immune from the Irish troubles and on 12 September 1880 an attempt was made to wreck the Down train near Bushey by means of a dynamite cartridge, which created such a small explosion that the driver thought it was a fog warning. The LNWR offered a reward of £100 to anyone who could provide information leading to the arrest of the offender, but the culprit was never caught. Activity by Fenians was at its height by 1881, as Irish nationalists sought independence from Britain, and many warnings were received during this period that threatened both the 'Irish Mail' and the Britannia Bridge, which was guarded by troops on several occasions. However, nothing actually happened, perhaps because of railway company employees' vigilance or press scaremongering.

Jim Roberts

Heading out of Conwy with the Down 'Irish Mail' is a rebuilt Caprotti valve-geared, large-boilered LNWR 'Claughton' class 4–6–0, *c.* 1928. When the LNWR won the entire mail contract between Euston and Kingstown in 1920 the 'Irish Mail' ran non-stop between Chester and Holyhead. The time allowed for the journey between these two points was 102 minutes for the day train in each direction, 103 minutes for the Down night train and 102 minutes for the Up night train. Many of these trains covered the distance in about 97 or 98 minutes, carrying an average load of 420 tons. They used 'George V' class 4–4–0s or 'Prince of Wales' class 4–6–0s, which were replaced in the 1920s by the 'Claughton' 4–6–0s that had originally been built for Euston–Glasgow expresses. As a prelude to non-stop running of the 'Irish Mail' between Euston and Holyhead the LMS ran a trial using an ex-LNWR 'Claughton' class 4–6–0. The train left Euston at 8.15 a.m. and arrived in Holyhead at 2.05 p.m.; David Noble was the driver and William Williams was the fireman.

D. Ibbotson

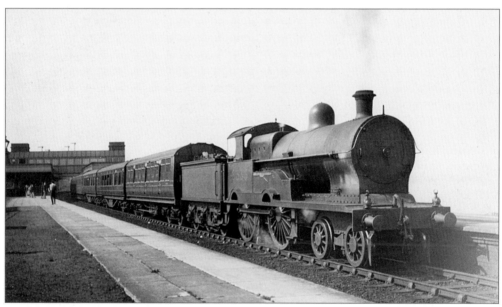

Ex-LNWR 'George V' class 4–4–0 as LMS No. 5335 heads the train through Colwyn Bay station on its way to Crewe, late 1920s. During the early years of the Grouping, ex-LNWR locomotives continued to operate the 'Irish Mail'.

Author's collection

Fowler-designed LMS 'Royal Scot' class 4–6–0 No. 6163 *Civil Service Rifleman* heads the Up 'Irish Mail' through Tamworth, 1931. Tamworth was the scene of an accident involving the 'Irish Mail' on 4 September 1870. There were two reasons for this: lack of signal and points interlocking (only partial at Tamworth) and the fact that two signal cabins that controlled the line at this point were out of sight of each other because the overbridge carrying the Midland Railway's Bristol–Derby main line bisected Tamworth station. The station had platform roads that were loops off the fast lines and the points controlling them were worked from the two signal-boxes. The 'Irish Mail' was some 13 minutes late as it approached Tamworth. The distant and outer home signals showed 'clear' as the train approached, so the driver kept the regulator open. The south box signalman was expecting the 'Mail' and set his road accordingly, which meant that the Up platform road was open to the sidings. The north box signalman was confused because his watch had stopped and he was expecting a goods train, so he had set his road for the Up platform. When he saw the light of the approaching 'Irish Mail' he thought it was a light engine. The 'Mail' ran over the crossover and through the Up platform road and along the dead end siding and went through the stop block at the end of the siding and landed upright in the river. One passenger and the driver were killed, and the guard was seriously injured.

Author's collection

LMS 'Royal Scot' No. 6161 *Kings Own* hauls the Up 'Irish Mail' towards Llandegai Tunnel, *c.* 1931. Until introduction of the Fowler 'Royal Scot' 4–6–0s on the 'Irish Mail' service in 1930, locomotives were changed at Crewe. From 1912 C.J. Bowen-Cooke's 'Claughton' class 4–6–0s worked the 'Irish Mail' from Euston to Crewe only, as the Chester to Holyhead section was not of a sufficiently high standard to take them until after the First World War, with 'George V' or 'Prince of Wales' locos taking over for the remainder of the journey to Holyhead. The introduction of 'Royal Scots' on Euston–Glasgow trains in 1927 released 'Claughtons' to work the 'Irish Mail' all the way from Euston to Holyhead as double home turns. In those days, the 'Irish Mail' train would often weigh something in the region of 420 tons.

H.A. Coulter

LMS 'Royal Scot' 4–6–0 No. 6159 *The Royal Air Force* heads the Down 'Irish Mail' through Bangor station *c.* 1933. A Webb coal tank can be seen on the right, possibly on shunting duties. By 1938 these engines were hauling trains of sixteen or seventeen coaches, a gross loaded weight of some 540 tons, unchanged from Euston to Holyhead on the day service. While services were not as fast between London and Dublin as they had been in LNWR days, train loads were some of the heaviest handled by an unaided 'Scot' anywhere on the LMS. Allowing for lengthy station stops for interchange of mail, the 'Irish Mail' was quick by the standards of the day. Its load of about 540 tons had to be moved over the 263½ miles between Holyhead and London in 285 minutes, with the last 82 miles from Rugby to London to be covered in 82 minutes. The summer of 1939 saw the fastest day 'Irish Mail' when the distance from Euston to Holyhead was covered in 293 minutes, at an average speed of 54 mph.

H.A. Coulter

LMS 'Royal Scot' No. 6113 *Cameronian* hauls the Up 'Irish Mail' near Gaerwen, Anglesey, 1934.

H.A. Coulter

LMS 'Royal Scot' No. 6162 *Queen's Westminster Rifleman* heads the Down 'Irish Mail' through Conwy, 1934. Despite the effects of the Great Depression between the First and Second World Wars the 'Irish Mail' continued to be well used, with services being accelerated in 1934, at a time when the railway companies were intensely competitive. The LMS was competing with the GWR for Irish traffic, who were carrying passengers via their harbour at Fishguard, although this service really covered a different area of Ireland. Down 'Irish Mail' services, between Euston and Dublin, were cut to 9 hours 15 minutes for the day service and 9 hours 50 minutes for the night service. Up 'Irish Mail' trains were allowed 9 hours 10 minutes for day services and 9 hours 20 minutes for night trains.

H.A. Coulter

Holyhead locoshed provided engines for Up 'Irish Mail' trains and had an allocation of top-link LNWR and LMS locos for this service. Here 'Royal Scot' locomotive No. 6159 *The Royal Air Force* is being prepared for 'Irish Mail' service during the summer of 1934.

H.A. Coulter

Royal Scot' No. 6135 *Samson* passes Penrhyn Sidings, Llandegai, with the Down 'Irish Mail', 1936.

H.A. Coulter

Royal Scot' No. 6125 *3rd Carbinier* is at the head of a relief 'Irish Mail' at Ty Croes, near Holyhead, 1936.

H.A. Coulter

At the head of another relief 'Irish Mail' as it approaches the Britannia Bridge is 'Royal Scot' No. 6101 *Royal Scots Grey, c.* 1937. By 1939 the Down 'Irish Mail' left Euston at 8.45 a.m. and made an extra stop at Watford to pick up outer suburban passengers. From Watford the train took 68 minutes to cover the 69.1 miles to Rugby. Halts of 9 minutes at Crewe and 8 minutes at Chester meant that the train arrived in Holyhead at 2.05 p.m. The night 'Irish Mail' left Euston at 8.50 p.m. and arrived in Holyhead at 2.20 a.m. the following morning, taking 5 hours 20 minutes to complete the whole journey. During the peak summer months relief 'Irish Mail' services left Euston some 5 minutes earlier and ran non-stop to Holyhead in 5¼ hours.

H.A. Coulter

Approaching Llandudno Junction, 'Royal Scot' No. 6118 *Royal Welch Fusilier* is seen at the head of the Down 'Irish Mail', *c.* 1934. Curving off to the extreme right of the picture is the branch line to the slate town of Blaenau Ffestiniog.

Peter Owen collection

Picking up mail at Bangor, the Up 'Irish Mail' is headed by 'Royal Scot' No. 6156 *The South Wales Borderer, c.* 1937. Up 'Irish Mail' trains were faster than the Down trains. The night train left Holyhead at 13 minutes past midnight and arrived in Euston at 5.30 a.m. The day service was fastest of all, taking only 5 hours 10 minutes from Holyhead to Euston. High-season relief 'Irish Mail' trains, running non-stop, reached Euston in 5 hours 3 minutes, with an average speed of 52.2 mph. Postal sorters had a busy time on Up trains, having to dispatch mail at speed at Bangor, Rhyl, Stafford, Tamworth, Nuneaton, Bletchley, Hemel Hempstead and Harrow.

H.A. Coulter

Leaving the Britannia Bridge at the head of the Up 'Irish Mail' shortly before the outbreak of the Second World War is 'Royal Scot' No. 6147 *The Northamptonshire Regiment.* The inscription above the portals shows that the bridge was built in 1850 and the engineer was Robert Stephenson, who was responsible for the construction of the whole of the Chester & Holyhead Railway. The bridge actually opened on 5 March of that year, and the first public train over it was the mail train from Chester, which crossed at 10.25 p.m. The first through train from Holyhead to Euston was the 2.30 p.m. from Holyhead on 18 March. This train actually had cheap excursion carriages attached so that some of the people from Holyhead could travel through the new tubes as far as Bangor and return on the 4.30 p.m. express.

H.A. Coulter

Approaching Colwyn Bay, 'Royal Scot' No. 6113 *Cameronian* is at the head of the Up 'Irish Mail', *c.* 1935. The war meant that the railway system was once again brought under government control, and speeds were cut to a maximum of 60 mph for all passenger trains in an effort to reduce maintenance requirements. By Whitsun 1940 maximum speeds were raised to 75 mph as the 'phoney war' progressed, but the invasion of the Low Countries by Germany forced railway speeds to be decelerated again. During the war only a day 'Irish Mail' operated, and night services were not restored until October 1946. Since then, except during the summer months, there has been only one sailing each way between Holyhead and Kingstown, or Dun Laoghaire as it has now become, in connection with 'Irish Mail' trains. The role of the railway has changed radically since the late 1930s, particularly with the construction of the new A55 expressway in the 1980s.

A.G. Ellis collection

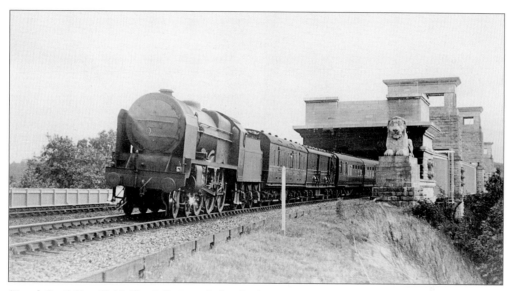

'Royal Scot' No. 6146 *The Rifle Brigade* heads the Up 'Irish Mail' out of the Britannia Bridge, mid-1930s. Unusually, the 'Irish Mail' was once stopped at Penmaenmawr during the war when a member of the local community was ordered to report to the War Office in London by 9 a.m. the following morning. By the time he had received the message it was too late for him to catch a train that would get him to his destination by the appointed time. The matter was mentioned to the local police sergeant who told him not to worry as arrangements would be made. A little later the gentlemen was told to go straight to the station where a train would be waiting for him. When he arrived there he found that the 'Irish Mail' had been specially ordered to stop and pick him up. He duly arrived at the War Office, feeling rather important, at 8 a.m. but was kept waiting until well after noon, which did much to deflate his ego.

Author's collection

Passing through Menai Bridge station, just before entering the Britannia Bridge, on its way to Holyhead is 'Royal Scot' No. 6139 *The Welch Regiment* at the head of the Down 'Irish Mail', late 1930s.

H.A. Coulter

Emerging from Penmaenrhos Tunnel, near Old Colwyn, 'Royal Scot' No. 6162 *Queen's Westminster Rifleman* is at the head of the Down 'Irish Mail', mid-1930s. Just east of this point is Llandulas, scene of the worst disaster to befall this famous train. On 26 August 1868 the Down 'Irish Mail' left Chester at 11.47 a.m. and at 12.24 p.m. a pick-up goods train, with two of its wagons loaded with casks of paraffin arrived at Llandulas sidings. Unfortunately, all of the goods train could not be accommodated in the sidings, but by dividing the train there was room for it to shunt clear. While the shunting operation was being prepared, the Down 'Irish Mail was due to pass through. While this took place, the rear six wagons were left on the main line, on a gradient of 1 in 147 and 1 in 100 falling towards Abergele. None of the wagon brakes were pinned down, except in the brake van. Three timber wagons were drawn out of the sidings and fly-shunted back on to the standing vehicles, with the brakesman running alongside attempting to apply the brakes. He failed and they hit the wagons on the main line, causing the brake cog on the brake van to fracture and all the wagons to run away towards Abergele. At 12.29 the 'Irish Mail' ran through Abergele station some 5 minutes late. Only 1¾ miles west of Abergele the driver saw the runaway wagons approaching, but by the time he realised what was happening, the wagons were almost upon the train. On impact the front of the 'Irish Mail' train was engulfed in paraffin and spilt coal from the loco's firebox caused the paraffin to ignite. The resulting fire consumed the first four coaches, all of which were locked in accordance with LNWR policy at this time, and the fireman and thirty-six passengers were killed.

D. Ibbotson

LMS class 4P Compound 4–4–0 locomotive pilots an unidentified 'Royal Scot' 4–6–0 on a Down relief 'Irish Mail' train at Britannia Bridge, *c.* 1935. These ex-MR engines appeared on the North Wales coast following the 1923 Grouping when ex-LNWR types began to be withdrawn.

Author's collection

It was not just 'Royal Scots' that were used on the relief 'Irish Mail' and here LMS Stanier class 5 4–6–0 No. 5311 is seen in charge of the Down relief 'Irish Mail' as it passes through Menai Bridge station on its way to Holyhead, *c.* 1937.

H.A. Coulter

An ex-LNWR 'George V' class 4–4–0 pilots an LMS 4P Compound 4–4–0 through Bangor station with the Up 'Irish Mail', mid-1930s.

H.A. Coulter

The doyen of the class, No. 6200 *The Princess Royal*, is seen with an Up 'Royal Scot' express as it enters Stafford station and gives an impression of what the 'Irish Mail' would have looked like with a 'Princess Royal' Pacific in charge during the wartime period. In April 1940 three 'Princess Royal' class locomotives, nos 6203, 6204 and 6205, were allocated to Holyhead and worked the 'Irish Mail'. This was a temporary move, no doubt brought about by the surplus of large locomotives as a result of the very much reduced train service, and they were moved from Holyhead early in November 1940.

Tim Shuttleworth collection

In the year of nationalisation and the train's centenary, 1948, the 12.50 Bangor–Euston train, headed by unrebuilt 'Royal Scot' No. 46140 *King's Royal Rifle Corps*, enters Chester station. Intensive use of the railways during the Second World War, lack of maintenance and a shortage of manpower left the system in a state of disrepair. Fixed structures and rolling-stock were particularly affected. The financial resources of the railway companies were drained and the government did not pay the companies the full value of the revenue that would have been earned during peacetime. In 1945 the new Labour government was committed to wholesale nationalisation of major industries and, despite vigorous opposition by the railway companies, the railways were nationalised from 1 January 1948. Thus the 'Irish Mail' passed from LMS control to State control, under the name of British Railways.

D. Ibbotson

The badly damaged 'Royal Scot' No. 46119 *Lancashire Fusilier*, August 1950. On 27 August 1950 the 'Irish Mail' was involved in a collision with a light engine at Penmaenmawr station at 3.05 a.m. As a result of the accident six people were killed and thirty-seven injured, and it was certainly due to the signalman's view being obstructed by the station foot-bridge. At 2.52 a.m. a light engine, class 5MT 2–6–0 'Crab' No. 42885, arrived tender first at the Down platform of Penmaenmawr station from Llandudno Junction. The Up 'Irish Mail', hauled by rebuilt 'Royal Scot' No. 46119 *Lancashire Fusilier* and running some 30 minutes late, had been accepted by the signalman at 2.50 a.m., just before the light engine arrived. No. 42885 crossed on to the Up line, whistled and waited to enter the sidings. The light engine did not set back into the sidings and crossed the points that had been set

for the expected 'Irish Mail'. The driver of No. 42885 moved forward and waited for the fireman to return. The fireman was waiting in the siding for the light engine to set back when he heard the 'Irish Mail' coming. The fireman waved his red lamp to warn the signalman that No. 42885 was still on the main line, and he immediately reset his signals to danger. The driver of No. 42885 realised what was going on and moved his engine forward in an effort to get clear of the following express. The 'Irish Mail' driver applied the brakes but was unable to prevent his train striking the light engine.

Author's collection

As *Lancashire Fusilier* struck the tender of No. 42885 it detached from its train and the brake coach pitched violently as it ran into the damaged track, rose into the air and plunged into the ballast. The damage to the leading coaches can be seen here. At the time of the crash a heavy goods train, loaded with explosives, was due from Llandudno Junction and the signalman immediately set the signals to danger on the Down line. The driver of the 'Irish Mail' sent the fireman to place detonators on the track to warn the driver of the goods train. He saw the signals change and, almost at once, heard the detonators and braked hard, stopping about 100 yd short of the coaches sprawled across the tracks. Fortunately, the goods engine suffered only slight damage as it brushed past the derailed *Lancashire Fusilier*.

Author's collection

The fifth, sixth and seventh coaches of the ill-fated 'Irish Mail' on the morning after the accident as cranes work to remove the wreckage. Immediately after the accident the signalman woke the stationmaster, who went to help, while his wife telephoned the emergency services. Local people came out to help, and the café opposite the station provided free tea and coffee for those involved. The station became a casualty clearing house until ambulances arrived. Repair gangs from Crewe and Chester worked to clear the line, and normal working was resumed within 30 hours of the accident. The Ministry of Transport inquiry into the accident concluded that the view from the signal-box, which was then situated at the west end of the station, while the sidings were at the east end, was obscured and hand signals could not easily be seen. This was an important factor when siding movements were controlled by hand or lamp signals, as they were at Penmaenmawr. Had BR not been planning to make changes to signalling at this time then the inquiry would almost certainly have insisted on a new signal-box at the eastern end of the station, opposite the sidings entrance. The busy nature of traffic here led the inquiry to consider the use of track circuiting and ground signals, which, if they had been in use, would have prevented the accident involving the 'Irish Mail'.

Author's collection

A year after the Penmaenmawr accident rebuilt 'Royal Scot' No. 46119 *Lancashire Fusilier* heads the Up day 'Irish Mail' through Penmaenmawr station, only a few yards from where the collision took place, summer 1951.

Gwyn Roberts

A Down relief 'Irish Mail', headed by rebuilt 'Royal Scot' No. 46149 *The Middlesex Regiment*, near Penmaenmawr, 25 May 1959.

Author's collection

The Up day 'Irish Mail', headed by rebuilt 'Royal Scot' No. 46150 *The Life Guardsman*, passes through the western end of Penmaenmawr, early 1950s. It was BR who introduced the locomotive headboard for the train after nationalisation. There is a story that two brothers from Holyhead worked as guards on the 'Irish Mail' but never met during thirty years' service on the train. This was because they worked on 'opposite' trains and only passed each other every day.

Author's collection

'Britannia' Pacific No. 70048 heads the Up 'Irish Mail' through the western end of Penmaenmawr during the summer, 1954. In 1953 five BR 'Britannia' Pacifics, nos 70030 to 70034 with BR1 tenders, were brought to Holyhead for use on 'Irish Mail' trains. The tenders were, however, too small for the demands of the service and were sent away to Longsight, Manchester, and were replaced in 1954 by engines nos 70045 to 70049, which had larger capacity BR1D tenders. From that time 'Britannia' Pacifics ran the 'Irish Mail' until they were replaced with diesel locomotives after the 1955 Modernisation Plan, which envisaged the replacement of steam by modern diesel and electric traction.

Gwyn Roberts

The same train passes Waverton, between Chester and Crewe, as it heads towards Euston. A year later the 'Irish Mail' was leaving Euston at 8.45 p.m. and Holyhead at 1.10 a.m. throughout the year; day 'Irish Mail' services operated in the summer only. Down 'Irish Mails' left Euston at 8.15 a.m. and the Up train left Holyhead at 1.25 p.m., Monday to Friday, and 4 p.m. on Saturday, all running non-stop between Chester and Holyhead. The night 'Irish Mail' from Euston connected with the 3.25 a.m. boat from Holyhead to Dun Laoghaire and the summer day train connected with the afternoon boat. The Saturday Up 'Irish Mail' took passengers from the same boat to Euston. The Up 1.10 a.m. night train took passengers off the night boat to Euston. All of these trains were hauled by 'Britannia' Pacifics.

S.D. Wainwright

Ex-LMS 'Princess Coronation' Pacific No. 46238 *City of Carlisle* heads the Up 'Irish Mail' through the eastern end of Penmaenmawr, early 1960s. With the demise of steam on the 'Irish Mail' service, following the 1955 Modernisation Plan, locomotives other than the 'Britannia' Pacifics could be found at the head of this famous train. The 'Princess Coronation' Pacifics had been transferred from the Euston–Glasgow route as diesel-electric traction took over and they lived out their lives on the North Wales coast. However, they were very rarely used on the 'Irish Mail' service, which makes this picture very unusual indeed.

Peter Owen

The demise of steam meant that 'Irish Mail' train services were accelerated to speeds that steam traction could not achieve. The first effect of this modernisation was the arrival at Holyhead of English Electric Type 4 (later class 40) diesel-electric locomotive No. D233 for training 'Irish Mail' drivers in November 1959. At the end of the same year five 'Britannia' Pacifics, based at Holyhead, were transferred to Crewe. Here, sister engine, No. D211, runs through Penmaenmawr before beginning operation on the 'Irish Mail' in 1964. From 25 April 1960 the 'Irish Mail' became fully dieselised.

Peter Owen

An unidentified English Electric Type 4 1Co–Co1 diesel-electric locomotive at the eastern end of Penmaenmawr with the Down 'Irish Mail', early 1960s. Known to enthusiasts as 'whistlers' because of the noise of the engine, these locos hauled the 'Irish Mail' all the way between Euston and Holyhead until the West Coast Main Line was fully electrified under the Modernisation Plan in 1966. From that time diesel locos operated between Holyhead and Crewe, with electric traction taking the 'Irish Mail' from Crewe to Euston. In the same period mail to Ireland was also being transported by air from Speke Airport, Liverpool. Naturally this took a fraction of the time the rail and sea method did, and the 'Irish Mail', therefore, assumed a lesser role in the transportation of mail.

Peter Owen

English Electric Type 4, now in BR blue, as class 40 No. 40024 *Lucania* arrives at Holyhead with what appears to be the 'Irish Mail', September 1978. It was, in fact, an unnamed express with just the nameboard, now privately owned, attached. By 1975 the Down night 'Irish Mail' departed Euston at 8.55 p.m. and ran non-stop to Holyhead, apart from a halt at Crewe to change from electric to diesel traction. It included sleeping cars and a miniature buffet, but no sorting coaches. The train reached Holyhead at 1.44 a.m., a total journey time of 4 hours 49 minutes. A supplementary train ran from Euston at 9.20 p.m. and called a Rugby, Crewe, Chester and Bangor to pick up and drop mail; the total journey time was just over 5 hours. The Up night 'Irish Mail' left Holyhead at 1.10 a.m., stopped at Bangor, Chester, Crewe and Rugby and reached Euston at 6.11 a.m. Daytime 'Irish Mails' ran during the summer season only. A relief train left Euston at 8.15 a.m., called at Crewe only and arrived in Holyhead some 4 hours later. The 'Irish Mail' with restaurant cars left Euston at 8.45 a.m., called at Watford, Rugby, Crewe and Chester and arrived in Holyhead at 1.17 p.m. Services from Holyhead were the relief 'Irish Mail' which left at 4.05 p.m., stopped at Crewe and arrived at Euston at 8.38 p.m. The 'Irish Mail' itself left Holyhead at 4.30 p.m., made the intermediate stops and arrived at Euston at 8.46 p.m.

Ron Watson-Jones

From 1979 Brush Type 4 (class 47) Co-Co diesel-electric locomotives began to operate the 'Irish Mail' between Crewe and Holyhead as the class 40s were retired and one can be seen at the head of an Up 'Mail' passing the granite sidings at Penmaenmawr, late 1980s. By the summer of 1986 the day 'Irish Mail' was not running. The night train left Euston at 10 p.m. on weekdays and Sundays, arriving at Holyhead at 2.28 a.m. On Saturdays the train left Euston at 9.45 p.m. and arrived at Holyhead at 2.41 a.m. The Up 'Mail' left Holyhead at 1.15 a.m., arriving at Euston at 6.14 a.m. On Sundays the train left Holyhead at 1 a.m., subject to the punctual arrival of the connecting boat, and arrived at Euston at 6.51 a.m. In 1987 the day 'Irish Mail' was reinstated and both trains stopped at Bangor, Llandudno Junction, Chester and Crewe, with a total journey time of about 4½ hours. In 1988 the Llandudno Junction stop was eliminated and in 1985 an additional stop was made at Nuneaton. In 1990–1 the winter timetable showed a night train only. The Down 'Irish Mail' left Euston at 10 p.m. and called at Milton Keynes, Rugby, Stafford, Crewe, Chester and Bangor, arriving at Holyhead at 2.35 a.m. The Up 'Irish Mail' left Holyhead at 2.15 a.m. and called at Bangor, Chester, Crewe, Rugby and Milton Keynes, arriving at Euston at 7.19 a.m. There was no service on Sundays.

Gwyn Roberts

Leaving Holyhead with the 13.15 Up 'Irish Mail' is BR class 47 Co-Co locomotive No. 47489, 31 December 1986. The train, made up of grey/blue and the new 'raspberry ripple' coaching stock, has just passed Holyhead signal-box and is at the entrance to Holyhead locoshed, which has an allocation of other class 47 engines within its confines.

Norman Kneale

Steam traction returned to the North Wales coast, between Crewe and Holyhead, from the summer of 1989 when BR began operating steam excursions after the route was 'steam approved'. Here, in the early 1990s, preserved BR 'Britannia' class Pacific No. 70000 *Britannia* herself is climbing away from Holyhead on such an excursion and carrying the 'Irish Mail' headboard above the smokebox door. The scene is reminiscent of the glorious days of steam in the 1950s when this class of engine was a regular performer on this famous old train.

Gwyn Roberts

Richard Branson's Virgin Trains took over the franchise for the West Coast Main Line, which included 'Irish Mail' services, following privatisation of the railway system in 1997. The train was operated by ex-BR Inter-City 125 sets, which were repainted in the Virgin livery of red, black and white. On the evening of 31 July 1998 Virgin Trains were involved in the 150th anniversary celebrations of the 'Irish Mail' when the first journey was re-enacted. Before the 7.10 p.m. 'Irish Mail' left Euston, IC125 power car No. 43101 was named the 'Irish Mail' and spectators dressed as people on the day of the departure of the first 'Irish Mail' would have done. Here, at Euston, Robert Stephenson, engineer of the Chester & Holyhead Railway, and Thomas Brassey, the contractor who built the line, are represented, as well as an 1848 Post Office employee.

Colin Marsden

Power car No. 43101 with its 'Irish Mail' name rests at Holyhead before returning to Euston with the Up 'Irish Mail', 1 August 1998. To complete the re-enactment, a watch, set to Greenwich Mean Time, was carried on the Stena Line ship HSS *Explorer*, which also carried mail brought from Euston on the 150th anniversary 'Irish Mail' of the previous evening. Both the watch and the mail were officially handed over at a special ceremony at Dun Laoghaire and a plaque to commemorate the anniversary was unveiled at Holyhead before the Up 'Irish Mail' left for Euston at 1.38 p.m. It is hoped that Virgin Railways will introduce new high-speed diesel trains for the 'Irish Mail' service in 2002, which will be able to 'tilt' and run at speeds up to 125 mph, although there have been demands in recent years to have the line between Crewe and Holyhead electrified. In any event, the future of this famous train seems to be secure.

Colin Marsden

As there was no Britannia Bridge across the Menai Strait in 1848, the 'Irish Mail' terminated at Bangor and passengers crossed into Anglesey over Thomas Telford's suspension bridge to Llanfair PG by stagecoach. The 1998 re-enactment included a stagecoach connection to Anglesey, although the scheduled 'Irish Mail' continued its journey to Holyhead. The stagecoach is seen crossing the Menai suspension bridge on the night of 31 July 1998.

Colin Marsden

CHAPTER TWO

THE ROUTE

The famous Doric arch entrance to Euston station in 1838, when the London & Birmingham Railway first opened. In 1963 the arch was demolished when a new Euston station was built as part of the West Coast Main Line electrification scheme. In 1848, ten years after the L&B opened Euston station, the first 'Irish Mail' train left the terminus at 8.45 p.m. on 31 July. The train reached Bangor at 5.25 a.m. and Holyhead at 9 a.m. Despite what appears to be a very slow time by today's standards, it was a revolution when compared to the timings stagecoaches were capable of achieving, and the journey was a lot safer as there was little risk of attack from highwaymen. In those days there was no such thing as heated carriages, but passengers could obtain footwarmers. On 'Irish Mail' services these were filled with sodium acetate which, when cold, could be shaken to regenerate heat.

National Railway Museum

The 'Irish Mail' begins its journey in the heart of Britain's capital city, at Euston, and ends in far North West Wales, on the Island of Anglesey, at Holyhead. In between it runs through industrial and urban landscapes, the soft country of the Home Counties, through Buckinghamshire, Northamptonshire, Warwickshire, Staffordshire and Cheshire, and the semi-industrial areas of North East Wales, and past the spectacular mountain scenery of Snowdonia. It runs from deep inland, through famous towns, to popular seaside resorts and terminates at one of the most important ports for boats to Ireland.

Starting on the London & Birmingham Railway, opened throughout in 1838, the 'Irish Mail' runs as far as Rugby and then traverses the much fought over Trent Valley Railway to Stafford. From Stafford, this famous train runs over the Grand Junction Railway as far as Crewe. This line opened in 1837 and linked the Liverpool & Manchester Railway (opened in 1830), at Newton Junction, with Birmingham, where it connected with the L&B. The Secretary of the GJR, Captain Mark Huish, played an important role in the development of the railways in this area, and was the driving force behind the establishment of the London & North Western Railway. From Crewe the 'Irish Mail' operated over the Chester & Crewe Railway, opened in 1840, to gain access to Chester, from where the train joined the Chester & Holyhead Railway, opened in 1848. Largely because of the machinations of Mark Huish, the L&B, GJR and M&BR were merged together to form the mighty London & North Western Railway in 1846. These railways are now part of the West Coast Main Line, which runs from Euston to Glasgow, and includes the section between Rugby and Stafford, via Birmingham, and was the first to be fully electrified using the 25 kv overhead system in the 1960s, with new stations being provided at Euston and Stafford. The C&HR remained independent until being absorbed by the LNWR in 1859. From that time the whole route of the 'Irish Mail' was under the control of the Euston company and, later, the LMS and BR (London Midland Region). Today express services over the WCML and the C&HR are in the hands of Richard Branson's Virgin Railways, while the infrastructure belongs to Railtrack following the end of British Railways in 1994.

With so many different companies responsible for constructing the railways over which the 'Irish Mail' has travelled, station architecture is as varied as the landscapes through which the train passes. Also, the variety of traction used on trains that have passed by the 'Irish Mail' over the years is of interest. From LNWR locomotives to modern BR traction, and top-link express engines to humble goods locos – all provide a background to the story of the 'Irish Mail'.

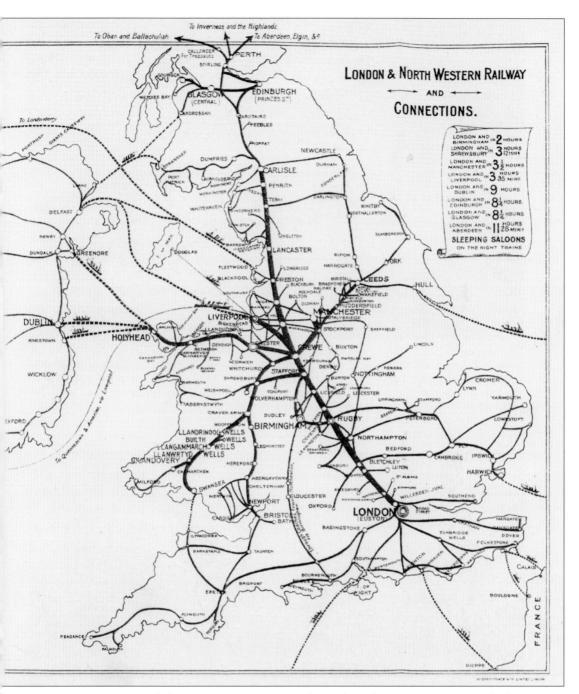

A map of LNWR main lines and their connections, *c.* 1905. The 'Irish Mail' route is clearly marked, showing the packet boat routes to Kingstown and Dublin. In those days the mail boats were operated by the City of Dublin Steam Packet Company, while the LNWR operated boats to Dublin (North Wall).

Author's collection

The interior of Euston station with LMS Fowler 'Patriot' class 4–6–0 No. 5532 *Illustrious* at the head of an express from Birmingham (New Street), 12 December 1938. This is how the station appeared to 'Irish Mail' passengers until it was totally rebuilt as part of the electrification project in the 1960s. The overall iron and glass roof was swept away in the name of progress and replaced by an anonymous concrete and glass 'antiseptic' Euston station.

H.C. Casserley

An ex-LNWR 'George V' class 4–4–0 as LMS No. 25348 is on an Up goods train at Camden goods depot, 1937. On leaving Euston station the 'Irish Mail' climbs Camden Bank, a hard ascent in steam days, with banking assistance provided, although modern traction takes the bank as if it does not exist.

Roger Carpenter collection

At the top of Camden Bank, on the left and opposite Camden Goods Depot, was Camden locoshed, which closed on 3 January 1966; it supplied motive power for expresses from Euston, including the 'Irish Mail'. The original shed, opened by the London & Birmingham Railway, is seen here with locomotives designed by Edward Bury, 2–2–0s with haycock fireboxes of 1837 design. Camden shed always had an allocation of top-link express locomotives for the famous expresses that ran from Euston, from LNWR types, through LMS Pacifics and 'Royal Scots' for the 'Irish Mail' service, to BR 'Britannia' Pacifics, which also found their way on to the Holyhead services, including the 'Irish Mail'. As the allocation for 30 January 1954 shows below, the shed had a large number of 'Royal Scot' locomotives for the 'Irish Mail' service.

National Railway Museum

Code 1B.
Ex-LMS 'Patriot' class 4–6–0: 45514 *Holyhead*, 45522 *Prestatyn*, 45523 *Bangor*, 45532 *Illustrious*, 45545 *Plantet*.
Ex-LMS 'Jubilee' class 4–6–0: 45592 *Indore*, 45601 *British Guiana*, 45603 *Solomon Islands*, 45669 *Fisher*, 45672 *Anson*, 45676 *Codrington*, 45686 *St Vincent*, 45735 *Comet*, 45736 *Phoenix*, 45740 *Munster*.
Ex-LMS 'Royal Scot' class 4–6–0: 46100 *Royal Scot*, 46116 *Irish Guardsman*, 46126 *Royal Army Service Corps*, 46139 *The Welch Regiment*, 46141 *The North Staffordshire Regiment*, 46142 *The York and Lancaster Regiment*, 46144 *Honourable Artillery Company*, 46147 *The Northamptonshire Regiment*, 46154 *The Hussar*, 46162 *Queen's Westminster Rifleman*, 46168 *The Girl Guide*, 46170 *British Legion*.
Ex-LMS 'Princess Coronation' class 4–6–2: 46229 *Duchess of Hamilton*, 46236 *City of Bradford*, 46237 *City of Bristol*, 46239 *City of Chester*, 46240 *City of Coventry*, 46141 *City of Edinburgh*, 46244 *King George VI*, 46245 *City of London*, 46247 *City of Liverpool*, 46249 *City of Sheffield*, 46250 *City of Lichfield*, 46253 *City of St Albans*, 46254 *City of Stoke-on-Trent*, 46256 *Sir William A. Stanier FRS*, 46257 *City of Salford*.
Ex-LMS 3F 0–6–0T: 47350, 47354, 47356, 47358, 47359, 47467, 47522, 47527, 47529, 47667, 47668, 47669, 47671.
Total 55.

Along with the 'Royal Scots', which operated the 'Irish Mail' until replaced by BR 'Britannia' Pacifics in the same year, many of the engines allocated at Camden were used on other express trains to the North Wales coast, even the 'Princess Coronation' Pacifics would appear at the head of North Wales services, including the 'Irish Mail', in the early 1960s.

Ex-LNWR 'Experiment' class 4–6–0 No. 5459 *City of Lichfield* (LNWR No. 165) at Willesden shed, September 1927. From Camden the 'Irish Mail' passes through the 1,220 yd Primrose Hill Tunnel and past stations at South Hampstead, Kilburn High Road, Queens Park and Kensal Green before approaching Willesden Junction. The original locoshed here closed on 27 September 1965 and was replaced by an electric depot on the Up side. Willesden freightliner terminal is now on the site of the steam locoshed.

Author's collection

Ex-LNWR 'Cauliflower' 0–6–0 goods engine No. 8441 (LNWR No. 348) in Willesden shed yard, 1937. At Willesden the Richmond–North Woolwich line crosses the WCML with a high-level station. The DC electric lines are on the east side of the main lines with an island platform station and are served by trains from Euston to Watford, operated by Silverlink Train Services, and also by Bakerloo underground trains from Elephant & Castle and Harrow & Wealdstone. The DC lines burrow under the main lines to Watford Junction on the west side with a diversion from Bushey via Watford High Street. The DC lines are four-rail to Harrow and three-rail beyond.

Author's collection

LMS Stanier 'Black 5' 4–6–0 No. 4915 at the head of a Down train, Watford Junction, 13 August 1949. After leaving Willesden, Wembley Stadium is passed near Wembley Central station. Shortly after passing Wembley Central the train crosses under the LNER ex-Great Central line from Manchester, Sheffield, Nottingham and Leicester to Marylebone, now served by Chiltern Trains from Birmingham Snow Hill, Banbury and Aylesbury via High Wycombe to Marylebone which then runs through South Kenton and Kenton. Between these two stations the Great Central's alternative route via Aylesbury and the underground Metropolitan line crosses over the WCML. Harrow on the Hill is to the west, where Thomas Port is buried in the local churchyard, the first engine driver to be killed on the London & Birmingham Railway on 7 August 1838. At Harrow & Wealdstone there was a major accident on 8 October 1952 when fog caused rebuilt 'Princess Royal' Pacific No. 46202 *Princess Anne*, the old 'Turbomotive', to be wrecked beyond repair, killing 112 people. After Harrow & Wealdstone the line passes stations at Headstone Lane, Hatch End, Carpenders Park and Bushey, where there were water troughs south of the station, and then enters Watford Junction. Watford Junction marks the end of the third-rail electric service from Euston, and is also the junction for branch lines to St Albans (Abbey) and Croxley Green and the main line to the north. The 'Irish Mail' then enters the 1 mile 57 yd Watford Tunnel and emerges into semi-rural landscape. On the left is the Grand Union Canal, which runs close to the railway as far as Rugby.

H.C. Casserley

Kings Langley station, 3 August 1957. Kings Langley has some significance for the 'Irish Mail' in that the nearby village of Bedmond was the birthplace of Nicholas Breakspear, the only English Pope. As Pope Adrian IV (1154–9) he issued a Papal Bull authorising the King of England to take possession of Ireland, which has led to so many problems between the islands.

H.C. Casserley

After Kings Langley the 'Irish Mail' passes Apsley station where one of the paper mills of John Dickinson, makers of Basildon Bond writing paper, is situated. The line then goes through a short cutting and on to a high embankment to reach Hemel Hempstead station. The station was previously known as 'Boxmoor' and went through various renamings becoming simply Hemel Hempstead on 20 December 1963. It was Hemel Hempstead and Boxmoor when this photograph was taken on 24 April 1962.

H.C. Casserley

An express, double-headed by ex-MR 4P 4-4-0 Compound No. 1018 and LMS 'Patriot' class 4-6-0 No. 5508, passes Boxmoor (Hemel Hempstead), 19 August 1939. Near Hemel Hempstead station is the grave of highwayman Bob Snooks, who robbed the mail in 1800. One of the letters contained about £500 in banknotes, a substantial amount in those days. By cashing one of these notes, suspicions were aroused and two years later, with a price of £300 on his head, Snooks was captured. He was hanged on 11 March 1802 and a headstone, erected in 1904, marks his grave. Transferring mail to the trains prevented such incidents and the 'Irish Mail' has never actually been robbed.

H.C. Casserley

Heading a Down express through Bourne End are ex-MR 4P 4–4–0 Compound No. 1092 and LMS 'Royal Scot' 4–6–0 No. 6138 *The London Irish Rifleman*, 11 July 1939. The train may be a relief 'Irish Mail' on its way to Rugby. When the 'Irish Mail' began operations, like other express trains, it had oil-lit carriages. However, from 1861 the 'Irish Mail' was the first LNWR train to have gas-lit carriages, such was its importance at that time. Six years after this photograph was taken Bourne End was the scene of an accident that killed forty-three passengers when the Perth–Euston express sleeping train crossed from the fast to slow line at excessive speed because of work being undertaken at Watford Tunnel.

H.C. Casserley

After Bourne End the 'Irish Mail' passes through Berkhamsted station, seen here with ex-LMS class 5 4–6–0 No. 44868 at the head of an Up parcels train, 5 September 1952.

H.C. Casserley

The Up 'Royal Scot', headed by a new 'Royal Scot' class 4–6–0, No. 6145, and without nameplates, passes through Berkhamsted, 28 March 1929. The 'Royal Scots' had been introduced on to Scottish expresses in 1927 and appeared on the 'Irish Mail' in 1930, having proved successful on other trains. The 'Royal Scots' also flourished on the 'Irish Mail', and were the main motive power on the Euston–Holyhead service for over twenty years.

Author's collection

At the head of the Down 'Royal Scot' is ex-LMS Stanier 'Princess Coronation' Pacific No. 46234 *Duchess of Abercorn* passing Northchurch, 9 April 1949. These Pacifics were sometimes used on 'Irish Mail' trains in the 1960s after withdrawal from Scottish services and replaced with modern diesel traction.

H.C. Casserley

Newly rebuilt 'Royal Scot' class 4–6–0 No. 46149 *The Middlesex Regiment*, yet to be fitted with smoke deflectors, on the Up fast line with an express train at Northchurch, 8 May 1948. Despite being the first year of BR ownership, the locomotive is still in LMS livery, although it has a BR number. After rebuilding 'Royal Scot' engines appeared on the 'Irish Mail' in just this condition.

H.C. Casserley

LMS 'Royal Scot' No. 6147 *Courier*, in original condition, passes Tring station at the head of a Down express, *c.* 1931. Tring lies at the summit of the line over the Chilterns, after which the line descends towards Cheddington.

Roger Carpenter collection

LMS 'Royal Scot' No. 6104 *Scottish Borderer*, also in original condition, passes Tring with an Up express, *c.* 1931. The Down 'Irish Mail' descends towards Cheddington, passing below five overbridges, the fourth of which carries the Icknield Way, a road more ancient than other Roman roads as it had previously been used by the ancient Britons. This road also marks the county boundaries of Hertfordshire and Buckinghamshire. After proceeding under the fifth bridge Cheddington station is reached, which was once a junction with a line from Aylesbury. After travelling under two further bridges Leighton Buzzard station, once a junction for Dunstable, is passed.

Roger Carpenter collection

After leaving Leighton Buzzard the 'Irish Mail' heads through the 283 yd Linslade Tunnel, seen here in 1958, as it heads towards Bletchley. This view shows the northern portals with, from left to right, the Up slow line, Down slow, Up fast and Down fast, the fast lines being those used by the 'Irish Mail' as it runs between Euston and Holyhead.

D. Ibbotson

Newton class 2–4–0 No. 2186 *Lowther* waits at Bletchley station, *c.* 1870. Note the road carriage on a flat wagon behind the locomotive at the head of the train. After passing through Linslade Tunnel the 'Irish Mail' enters Bletchley station, which was once an important junction, with lines to Oxford, linking up with the GWR, and to Cambridge and the LNER, until Dr Beeching had these lines closed. Today there is only a branch to Bedford, joining the ex-Midland Railway main line from St Pancras to Leicester.

Author's collection

Ex-LMS Stanier two-cylinder 4P 2–6–4 tank, looking rather grubby in its BR livery as No. 42582, waits at Bletchley station with a local train, possibly for the Cambridge line, given that the push-pull trailer is of LNWR origin, *c.* 1956. After leaving Bletchley the 'Irish Mail' passes through Milton Keynes as it heads towards Wolverton.

D. Ibbotson

An LNWR 0–6–0 'Special Tank' at Wolverton Works, 1960. The locomotive works of the London & Birmingham Railway was at Wolverton, and later became the LNWR Southern Division locoworks, where some of the McConnell 2–2–2 'Bloomers' were built. These engines hauled the 'Irish Mail' between Euston and Stafford, from where LNWR locos of the Northern Division took over for the journey to Chester and Holyhead. From 1862, when Ramsbottom took charge of LNWR locomotive affairs, all locomotive construction was concentrated at the Crewe works, while Wolverton dealt with carriages and wagons.

D. Ibbotson

Castlethorpe station, 20 August 1953. After leaving Wolverton, which once had a branch to Newport Pagnell, the 'Irish Mail' passes through Castlethorpe station, which closed on 7 September 1964. After travelling under six bridges and passing the now closed Roade station the train enters a walled cutting with the Northampton loop opened in 1881 dropping away to the east.

R.M. Casserley

Blisworth station, 1950s. A local train has recently arrived as there are passengers on the platform awaiting a connecting train. Blisworth was the junction for the L&B branch to Peterborough (1846) and to Northampton Castle, with pull-push service, which connected with some main-line trains from 1881. Stratford-upon-Avon and Midland Junction Railway trains to Banbury and Stratford/Broom Junction used their own separate terminus on the west of the main line until closure in 1952. The Northampton loop line rejoins the Euston–Crewe line just south of Rugby.

H.C. Casserley

The 492 yd Stowe Hill Tunnel, 1957. A further 6¾ miles from Blisworth, after the 'Irish Mail' has passed through the Stowe Hill Tunnel, once stood Weedon station, which boasted a branch to Daventry and Leamington Spa. Weedon was the scene of an accident involving the 'Irish Mail' on 14 August 1915. A taper pin, smaller than a pencil, designed to lock the screwed collar that retained the offside coupling rod, fell off the engine of the 8.45 a.m. Birmingham New St–Euston train on the Up line when the Down 'Irish Mail' was due. After the pin had dropped off, the collar unthreaded itself and the coupling rod then came off the crank pin, struck one of the sleepers of the Down line and put the track out of alignment. The Down 'Irish Mail' was approaching at speed and was derailed, with ten people killed and a further sixty-four passengers and railway staff injured. The accident inspectors suggested that the collars in question should, in future, have left- and right-hand threads so that, if a pin was lost, they could not unscrew themselves in this way.

D. Ibbotson

Kilsby Tunnel, 1957. After Weedon 5½ miles away was Welton station, which is just before the 'Irish Mail' enters the 1 mile 666 yd Kilsby Tunnel. It was flooded with water when it was under construction, and such were the problems with it that it was thought that it might have to be abandoned. In the event the tunnel was finished, although the estimated cost of £99,000 had increased to an actual figure of about £300,000, but it completed the link between London and Birmingham.

D. Ibbotson

After emerging from the Kilsby Tunnel, the 'Irish Mail' travels 4 miles north and enters Rugby station, seen here during the First World War with an LNWR local train in the distance. This is the station that had been built in 1881 to replace an earlier L&B structure. The opening of the Trent Valley Railway to Stafford in 1847 ensured the station's importance, and such a significant junction was supplied with its own locoshed, coded 2A, to supply motive power for trains from the Rugby Portland Cement Co's works on the Leamington line. Rugby was the scene of a boiler explosion on a locomotive that was hauling the 'Irish Mail' on the night of 8 July 1861. The loco, whose lower plates had become so corroded that they were only one-sixteenth of an inch thick, had been retubed some three years earlier. It appeared that no one had noticed the state of the boiler when this work was carried out. After leaving Rugby the train was approaching Easenhall Bridge when the boiler barrel failed and there was a terrific explosion. The engine virtually disintegrated, part of the boiler hit the parapet of the bridge and fell back into the tender. One of the driving wheels blew off and also hit the bridge, the crank axle broke, part of the framing and motion was thrown on to the Up line, and fragments of tubes, boiler laggings, sheeting, feedpipes and handrails were scattered on both sides of Easenhall Cutting for some distance. The explosion killed the fireman, but there were no other fatalities, which was surprising as the train was travelling at 40 mph at the time.

Author's collection

Shilton station, 1930s. After leaving Rugby the 'Irish Mail' passes through the site of Brinklow station before reaching Shilton station. As Shilton only served a small community its passenger services were sparse and it was closed, along with Brinklow, on 16 September 1957 before the Beeching proposals. After leaving Rugby the 'Irish Mail' travels on the Trent Valley Railway (TVR), which was first proposed by the Manchester & Birmingham Railway and interested the London & Birmingham because the new route would avoid Birmingham altogether. This alarmed the Grand Junction Railway's Secretary, Captain Mark Huish, who was aware that such L&B interest would deprive the GJR of traffic. In order to make life difficult for the L&B Captain Huish made an agreement with the GWR to provide broad gauge tracks from Rugby, via Birmingham, to Liverpool. This so alarmed the L&B, who were opposed to the broad gauge, that the company sought talks with the GJR. As a result the Trent Valley Railway was financed by the GJR, who obtained running powers under the TV Act of 1845. It was opened after the formation of the LNWR in 1847. The talks with the L&B led to the establishment of the LNWR and difficulties for the GWR as the Paddington company sought to compete with the LNWR for routes to Liverpool and Ireland.

Author's collection

After Shilton comes Bulkington, seen here during electrification of the West Coast Main Line in the 1960s. The station actually closed as early as 1931, although the building still remains. The nameboard in this picture is still in LNWR-style lettering.

Roger Carpenter collection

Some 14½ miles north of Rugby comes Nuneaton station, seen here with a tank engine in the distance, c. 1910. Although of only minor importance when the TVR first opened, Nuneaton was to develop into the most important junction on the route, receiving a line from Coventry in 1850, from Hinckley in 1862, extended to Leicester in 1864 and the Ashby and Nuneaton Joint Line north of the station in 1873, and Birmingham in Nuneaton Abbey Street. Such was its growing significance that the station was enlarged and partly rebuilt in 1909 as the station seen here. Today Nuneaton is still a junction, with lines to Coventry and Leicester from Birmingham. Trains were diverted via Nuneaton Trent Valley after closure of Abbey Street from 4 March 1965.

Author's collection

LNWR class B.4 cylinder 0–8–0 No. 1282 at Nuneaton locoshed yard, 1925. Nuneaton was provided with its own locoshed from 1878, a subshed of Rugby which was coded 2D to 8 July 1950, 2B to 9 September 1963 and finally 5E to closure on 6 June 1966.

Roger Carpenter collection

Ex-LMS Stanier three-cylinder 'Jubilee' class 4–6–0 No. 45584 *North-West Frontier* approaches Nuneaton, past Ashby Junction, with an express, probably from Manchester, 11 September 1954.

Roger Carpenter collection

From Nuneaton the 'Irish Mail' heads towards Atherstone station, some 5½ miles away, seen here after the TVR had been quadrupled in the early 1900s. A feature of the quadrupling was the signal-box, which was supported on girders after being placed in the centre of the four-track formation. Atherstone was one of the TVR first-class stations and was designed by J.W. Livock in a Jacobean style, as were all the first-class stations on the TVR. Up until the quadrupling, the TVR had to cross a level crossing here at a speed of no more than 4 mph. The LNWR obtained powers to build a bridge over the road and the Coventry Canal, which replaced the level-crossing in September 1903 and allowed trains to run at speed through Atherstone.

Author's collection

LNWR 'Jumbo' 2–4–0 No. 2194 *Cambrian* is at Tamworth station with a Down semi-fast train, 1925. Following Atherstone the TVR runs through to Tamworth, once the main junction for mail traffic, although the 'Irish Mail' never stopped here, the train just picking up mail from apparatus at speed. In its day mails from Euston to the north stopped at Tamworth to exchange mails. Mail trains to and from London, Scotland, Bristol, Lincoln and Newcastle converged at this point, the Midland Railway's Derby–Bristol main line crossing the LNWR at Tamworth. Nowadays the centre for mail trains has moved to Derby, not least because of its proximity to East Midlands Airport, used for the dispatch of air mail brought in by train.

Roger Carpenter collection

Leaving Tamworth with a Stafford local train is LMS class 2P 4–4–0 No. 40652, late 1950s. Tamworth is best known as the parliamentary seat of Sir Robert Peel, famous for his measures to improve the Metropolitan Police. He was also responsible for the re-introduction of the dreaded income tax and for the inauguration of free trade when he repealed the Corn Laws. Peel was also involved in the development of railways at Tamworth when he cut the first sod for the TVR on 13 November 1845.

Roger Carpenter collection

Approaching Tamworth in 1959/60 is an express double-headed by ex-LMS 'Patriot' class 4–6–0 No. 45510 and rebuilt 'Royal Scot' 4–6–0.

Roger Carpenter collection

Rugeley station, seen here before quadrupling, *c.* 1900. From Tamworth the TVR enters Lichfield station before Rugeley. While Rugeley is well known for the red oxide used as jewellers rouge, hence the name of the town, Lichfield is famous for its three-spired cathedral and for being the birthplace of Dr Samuel Johnson. At Lichfield the South Staffordshire Railway from Winchester Junction to Dudley crosses over the TVR with high-level platforms, now the terminus of the electric service from Redditch via Birmingham New St. There is an east to north curve allowing through running from Burton to Stafford.

Tim Shuttleworth collection

Entering Rugeley station at the head of a freight train is ex-LMS Hughes-Fowler 'Crab' 2–6–0 No. 42920, *c.* 1959. In the 1850s locals tried to have the town's name changed and asked the Prime Minister, who was not keen on the idea, to suggest a new name. He suggested his own name, Palmerston, but 'Palmer' had unfortunate associations for Rugeley. A Dr Palmer, who was renowned for poisoning his rich patients with strychnine, had been a resident in the town. Needless to say, the idea of a name change was dropped after Palmerston's suggestion.

The northern portal of the Shugborough Tunnel, 1960s. Some 2¾ miles from Rugeley is a junction of the North Staffordshire Railway line to Stoke-on-Trent at Colwich. There was once a station here, but it was closed on 3 February 1958. After Colwich the 'Irish Mail' enters the 700 yd Shugborough Tunnel.

D. Ibbotson

LNWR 'Dreadnought' Compound 2–2–2–0 No. 510 *Leviathan* is in steam at Stafford station, 1904. Stafford was the most important station on the GJR when it opened in 1837, eleven years before the 'Irish Mail' first ran. The 'Dreadnought' was often seen on the 'Irish Mail' in the late nineteenth and early twentieth centuries.

Roger Carpenter collection

Coming from Crewe, ex-LNWR 'Claughton' class 4–6–0 enters Stafford station, *c*. 1934. Stafford had branches to Uttoxeter and Wellington as well as the GJR and TVR and, as such, retained an important role. The line to Wellington is seen on the left, while the Great Northern Railway line to Uttoxeter, Derby and Nottingham is on the right. Both branches have now gone. Such was the importance of Stafford, it was provided with a locoshed, a subshed of Crewe, to provide motive power for expresses to Crewe and for local trains to Wellington. Stafford was also the home of locomotive and rolling-stock manufacturers W.G. Bagnall and Co. Ltd, whose products were exported all over the British Empire.

Tim Shuttleworth collection

As part of West Coast Main Line electrification Stafford station was totally rebuilt, although work was delayed for a while when the government became concerned about the escalating cost of electrification, leaving the station in a half demolished state. The completed station is seen here in the 1970s with the electric service fully operational.

Author's collection

Ex-LMS 'Patriot' class locomotive No. 45510, in BR green livery, approaches Great Bridgeford station with a 14-coach Glasgow–Birmingham train, 16 June 1951. From Stafford the 'Irish Mail' passes through the site of Great Bridgeford station, which was closed under the Beeching proposals. Beyond Great Bridgeford the M6 motorway crosses the GJR, followed by Norton Bridge station, a modern structure built as part of the electrification programme. Norton Bridge is the junction for the Potteries, the line going off to the right.

Tim Shuttleworth

Crewe South signal-box, designed in the 1930s, seen here in 1985. Some 19¾ miles from Norton Bridge is probably the most famous railway station in the world, Crewe. The 'Irish Mail' first passes the now long gone stations of Standon Bridge, Whitmore (where there were once water troughs), Madeley and Betley Road. The first sign that Crewe is close by is the sight of Basford Hall signal-box, after which extensive sidings fan out on the left and carriage sidings appear on the right. Basford Hall sidings contain many freight wagons and, as the train nears Crewe station, the modern locomotive depot comes into view, with electric and diesel locomotives stabled there.

Revd David Harvey

The interior of Crewe station with a train awaiting departure, c. 1900. The 'Irish Mail' has called at Crewe throughout most of its history, mainly for locomotive changes, except in the 1930s when the 'Royal Scot'-hauled train ran through non-stop. Crewe is very much a railway town, created by the GJR as the intermediate point between Warrington and Birmingham in 1837. Then known as Monks Coppenhall, only 184 people lived here, but by the 1940s the population had grown to 42,000. In 1903 the LNWR employed some 10,000 people at Crewe.

Author's collection

LNWR 'Waterloo' class 2–4–0 No. 742 *Spitfire*, *c.* 1900. Crewe was the centre of locomotive building from 1845, providing engines for the 'Irish Mail' services between Stafford and Holyhead. When McConnell resigned as Locomotive Superintendent of the Southern Division at Wolverton in 1861 all locomotive construction was undertaken at Crewe, with Ramsbottom in charge, from 1862. His 2–4–0 'Newton' class locomotives appeared on the 'Irish Mail', often double-headed, following withdrawal of his 'Lady of the Lake' class engines. Francis Webb succeeded Ramsbottom in 1871, and was responsible for construction of the 2–4–0 'Precedent' class, known as 'Jumbos', as well as 2–2–2–2 'Greater Britain' and 2–2–2–0 'Dreadnought' Compound locomotives. He also produced 4–4–0 'Benbow' class engines, all of which appeared on the 'Irish Mail'. In 1903 George Whale succeeded Webb as CME at Crewe and he introduced new designs that were destined to appear on the 'Irish Mail', including the 4–4–0 'Precursor' class in 1904, and the 4–6–0 'Experiment' class in 1905. C.J. Bowen-Cooke became CME in 1909 and three of his designs became regulars on the 'Irish Mail': in 1910 the 'Prince of Wales' class 4–6–0 appeared, along with his 4–4–0 'George V' class. In 1912 Bowen-Cooke introduced his 4–6–0 'Claughton' class, which was used on 'Irish Mail' services after the Grouping.

Roger Carpenter collection

LNWR 'Experiment' class 4–6–0 No. 1658 *Flintshire* pilots 'Claughton' class No. 209 *J. Bruce Ismay* on a Down express at Crewe, 1920. Crewe is a major junction of lines to Chester and North Wales, Glasgow and Manchester north of the station, and with Stoke-on-Trent, Derby, London and Shrewsbury south of the station.

Roger Carpenter collection

An unidentified LNWR 'Prince of Wales' class 4–6–0 is at the head of an Up express, *c.* 1920. These engines were a common sight on the 'Irish Mail' until replaced by LMS 'Royal Scots'.

Roger Carpenter collection

Another 'Prince of Wales' class 4–6–0, as LMS No. 5610 *Robert Southey*, heads an Up train out of Crewe, 1930. At about this time these engines were being replaced on the 'Irish Mail' with 'Royal Scot' 4–6–0s.

Roger Carpenter collection

An unnamed 'Claughton' class 4–6–0 No. 6029 at Crewe, May 1928. At this time they were at the head of 'Irish Mail' services between Crewe and Holyhead.

Roger Carpenter collectio

LNWR 'Prince of Wales' class 4–6–0 No. 28 at Crewe station, c. 1923. In 1985 Crewe station was extensivel remodelled, resulting in virtual closure while this work was carried out. During this period 'Irish Mail' train underwent locomotive changes at Stafford, recalling the days before 1862 when engines for the 'Irish Mail' wer changed from Southern to Northern Division engines here. The benefits of the Crewe remodelling included muc faster running of through trains.

Roger Carpenter collectio

Ex-LNWR 'Precursor' class 4–4–0 as LMS No. 25304 *Greyhound* pilots a rebuilt 'Royal Scot' 4–6–0 No. 6157 *The Royal Artilleryman* at Crewe, 1946. The pairing shows an engine which had control of the 'Irish Mail' until replaced by the 'Royal Scot' class.

Roger Carpenter collection

Ex-LNWR 'Prince of Wales' class 4–6–0 No. 25631 (LNWR No. 1400) *Felicia Hemans* at Crewe North shed yard, c. 1930. Crewe North provided locomotives for 'Irish Mail' trains running between here and Euston or Holyhead, and also supplied express motive power for a variety of passenger trains out of Crewe.

Author's collection

Ex-LNWR 'Claughton' class 4–6–0 LMS No. 5994 (LNWR No. 6) at Crewe North shed, July 1933.
Author's collection

Ex-LNWR 0–8–0 No. 49267 awaiting scrapping at Crewe locomotive works, 3 February 1963. On leaving Crewe the 'Irish Mail' takes the line to Chester past the old Crewe North signal-box, which is now part of the Crewe Heritage Centre where steam locos are kept for excursions along the North Wales coast. The centre is on the site of the old locomotive works, which were demolished when Crewe station was remodelled. Soon afterwards the 'Irish Mail' passes under Eagle Bridge, where four spread eagles are perched on shields displaying the initial 'C'. The letter does not, however, stand for Crewe, but for 'Conwy' (on the North Wales coast) from where the eagles had come as scrap iron from disused wagons. An engineer took pity on them, saved them from being melted down and had them mounted here. Overhead wires come to an end on the outskirts of Crewe, which explains why diesel haulage has to be used for the remainder of the journey.
Author's collection

Calveley station, in derelict condition, looking towards Crewe, 1977. Today there are no stations between Crewe and Chester, where once there were five: at Worleston, Calveley, Beeston Castle, Tattenhall Road and Waverton. At Calveley the railway runs close to the Shropshire Union Canal, once owned by the LNWR/LMS.

N. Mundy

LNWR 'Waterloo' class 2–4–0 No. 763 *Violet* at the Warrington end of Chester station, *c.* 1920.

Roger Carpenter collection

LMS 'Black 5' 4–6–0 No. 5151 waits at Chester station, 7 July 1935. This locomotive would have been new at this time.

A.G. Ellis collection

Tank engines of the GWR, 'Prairie Tank' No. 5179 and LMS No. 40110, stand under the overall roof at Chester station, which was partly removed in the 1960s and replaced with platform canopies, 1950s. Chester station had become an important junction by 1840, when the Chester & Birkenhead Railway and Chester & Crewe Railway were opened, and it was this fact that, along with the existing port at Holyhead, convinced the authorities that the coastal route between the two points would be ideal as the link to Ireland. Another company, the Shrewsbury & Chester Railway, opened its line in 1846, gaining access to Chester station over the, as yet, incomplete Chester & Holyhead Railway from Saltney Junction. It was an agreement between the CHR and S&CR that allowed development of the station site. The absorption of the CHR by the LNWR and S&CR by the GWR brought Chester under joint ownership.

D. Ibbotson

An ex-GWR 2–6–2 tank is bringing in the Birkenhead–Paddington express at Chester, an express 4–6–0 being put on here, while ex-GWR Collett 'Grange' class 4–6–0 No. 6869 *Resolven Grange* departs with a train for Shrewsbury, 1952. At Shrewsbury the train will connect with services for the Cambrian Coast Line to Aberystwyth and Pwllheli. Originally the Cambrian Railways had been devised to compete with the LNWR port at Holyhead by building its own line through to Porth Dinllaen, near Caernarfon (the port suggested by Charles Vignoles in his original survey), but the mighty LNWR applied enough pressure to prevent this happening. In the event, the Cambrian line never got any further than Pwllheli and did not become a financial success, possibly because it could not realise its dream of establishing its own port for Ireland.

D. Ibbotson

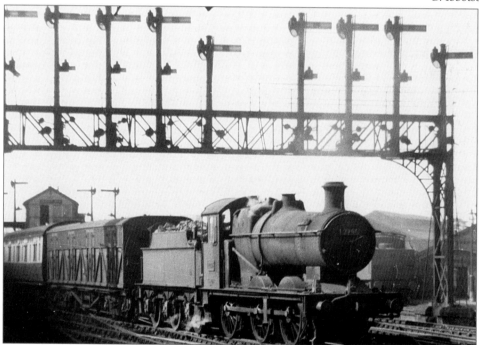

An ex-GWR 'Collett Goods' 0–6–0 No. 2299 arrives in Chester with an empty stock train from Wrexham, 1952. The LNWR did face some competition for Irish traffic, with the GWR operating train and boat services from Milford Haven and, from 1907, Fishguard in South Wales to ports in the far south of Ireland; GWR trains also carried mails from here. However, Holyhead remained the most prominent port for Ireland because of its proximity to Dublin.

D. Ibbotson

A Down Holyhead express, possibly the 'Irish Mail', for Holyhead with an ex-LNWR 'Prince of Wales' class 4–6–0 at the head exits the west portals of Northgate Tunnel, *c.* 1920. On the 'Welsh Curve' the 'Irish Mail' enters a series of broad tunnels cut into the sandstone, and originally, as in this view, the tunnels carried four tracks, but this has now been cut to two.

D. Ibbotson

On leaving Chester station the 'Irish Mail' takes the 'Welsh Curve', passing the GWR shed, now a diesel depot, seen here on the right in 1958. The GWR had a shed here to provide express motive power for Birkenhead–Paddington expresses. The line to Hooton, on the Wirral, which is now fully electrified, branches off to the right and takes passengers to Liverpool. A single track, linking the 'Welsh Curve' with the line to Liverpool, trails off to the right and forms a triangle on which steam locomotives turn when on excursions between Hereford and Chester.

Roger Carpenter collection

After departing from Chester the 'Irish Mail' travels 2 miles to Saltney Junction and then just beyond here reaches Saltney Ferry, seen here in 1960. The station served a branch to Mold, which continued to Denbigh on the Rhyl–Corwen route; Chester to Denbigh closed on 30 April 1962. At Saltney Junction the ex-GWR (S&C) line to Wrexham, Shrewsbury and Birmingham (Snow Hill) branches off to the left. Gone are the days when GWR 'Star', 'Castle' and 'County' class 4–6–0s ran Birkenhead–Paddington expresses along this route, withdrawn in March 1967. Nowadays only DMU services operate between Chester and Wolverhampton on a single line as far as Wrexham.

Author's collection

Departing from Chester with a Llandudno-bound excursion is ex-LNWR 'George V' class 4–4–0 LMS No. 5303, 1930s. After the second tunnel, a three-rise lock of the Shropshire Union Canal is passed on the left. The 'Irish Mail' then runs over a high embankment and 49-arch Roodee Viaduct, past Chester racecourse, on the left, and on to the Dee Bridge. Opened in 1846, the original bridge collapsed in May 1847 under a Shrewsbury to Chester train, killing six passengers. A cast-iron replacement, designed by Robert Stephenson, was opened in the same year, but was

found to be of bad design and in 1871 the structure had to be extensively rebuilt of wrought iron and brick. The widening of the railway at Saltney Junction, authorised by an Act of 1893, allowed the GWR to build a widening structure next to the bridge, opened in 1904. This section, nearest to the racecourse, is still in use, while the original section was closed to traffic, under rationalisation at Chester, in 1979.

Author's collection

Near to Saltney Ferry station a noticeboard marked the border between England and Wales, seen here in the 1950s. The sign has since disappeared.

Author's collection

The eight-road locoshed, seen here with its allocation of goods engines used for handling traffic from the nearby marshalling yard at Mold Junction, near Saltney Ferry, 1950s. The shed was also used by ex-GWR locos when its shed at Chester was closed, and this shed was closed on 18 April 1966 and the site is now used by a scrap merchant. The marshalling yard at Mold Junction closed in 1964.

Roger Carpenter collection

Sandycroft station, seen here shortly before closure in May 1961. After leaving Mold Junction the 'Irish Mail' passes close to Hawarden, home of the nineteenth-century Prime Minister and statesman William Gladstone. When the CHR was under construction an agreement was made with Gladstone to use some of his land. In exchange for this he made the condition that he would be able to board the 'Irish Mail' in his fields in order to attend Parliament in London; he would notify the railway company at what time he wished to travel and the guard would carry a short ladder to enable him to get on the train. In 1884 Sandycroft station was opened nearby and Gladstone was able to board his train there. Between Mold Junction and Sandycroft lies Chester airport and aircraft works on the left of the railway.

Author's collection

A rather unkempt ex-LMS class 5 4–6–0 at the head of a freight train for Mold Junction at Shotton station, mid-1950s. After leaving Sandycroft the 'Irish Mail' passes Queensferry, the first of the original 1848 stations on the CHR from Chester. Queensferry closed on 14 February 1961, and nothing of it now remains. After Queensferry, Shotton steelworks, established by John Summer Ltd, comes into view. In its heyday the works employed some 6,000 people and had about 45 miles of railway on the site. The works is served by Shotton station, which is reached after the 'Irish Mail' passes under the ex-Great Central Railway line from the Wirral to Wrexham and site of Shotton High Level station. The present station, opened in August 1972, was built between the platforms of the original station, which opened in April 1907 and was known, from 1952, as Shotton Low Level. This original station was closed in 1966 and the new station reverted to the original name of 'Shotton'.

Gwyn Roberts

Connah's Quay station, *c.* 1900. A little beyond Shotton lies the old Connah's Quay goods shed where, from 1906, the quadruples section from Saltney Junction ended. In recent years rationalisation has reduced the line back to double track. After passing the site of Crumps Wagon Repair Works, on the right, the 'Irish Mail' enters the site of Connah's Quay station, which closed in 1966. Opened in 1870, the station was known for its connection with the Wrexham, Mold and Connah's Quay Railway.

Author's collection

Connah's Quay station looking towards Chester, August 1953. The old LMS nameboard is still *in situ.*

R.M. Casserley

The 98 yd Rocklifee Hall Tunnel under which the 'Irish Mail' passes before it approaches Flint station, 1960s.

D. Ibbotson

Flint station looking towards Holyhead, 1960s. Flint was a busy port, supplying Muspratt's chemical works, the largest employer in the area. The station retains its original Francis Thompson-designed buildings, Thompson being the architect for stations on the CHR, and remains open today. On entering Flint station (now spelt Fflint) the remains of the Plantagenet castle that once stood on the bank of the River Dee can be seen.

Author's collection

Mostyn station, 20 miles beyond Chester, with the iron works in the background, 1960s. Just beyond Flint the CHR was quadrupled as far as Llandulas between 1896 and 1915. Now only double track, the 'Irish Mail' runs on a virtually straight course past marshland at the mouth of the River Dee, and in the right distance is the Wirral. Some 2 miles west of Flint lies the remains of Bagillt station, closed in 1966 and once situated in the middle of Bettisfield Colliery. A couple of miles further and Holywell station, which closed in 1966, is passed. Holywell was once a junction with a little branch to Holywell Town, the site of St Winifride's Well; the branch was closed in 1954. Next the site of Mostyn station, which closed in May 1964, is reached. This station had four platforms and sidings that served Mostyn Docks, which remain in use today. Just before Mostyn station an old Heysham–Belfast ferry, the *Duke of Lancaster*, is beached and is currently used as an entertainment centre. Just 3 miles west of Mostyn is the site of Point of Ayr Colliery, recently closed, the last deep mine in North Wales to be worked. Immediately afterwards the remains of Talacre station, opened in 1903 and closed in May 1964, are passed. The 'Irish Mail' then takes a long curve as the mouth of the Dee empties into the Irish Sea, which 'Irish Mail' passengers will soon cross to reach Dublin. This is the end of the industrialised section of the North Wales coast and the landscape is now dotted with holiday caravans.

Author's collection

Prestatyn, the first station in the holiday region of the North Wales coast, 1977. Prestatyn once had a little branch line to Dyserth, but this closed to passengers on 22 September 1930 and freight on 4 May 1964, except for private sidings that closed on 8 September 1973.

N. Mundy

The layout of the track at the Holyhead end of Rhyl station, 1960s. Just 3¾ miles from Prestatyn lies Rhyl, an important holiday centre and a big revenue earner on the CHR. The station also served a branch to Denbigh that opened in October 1858 and closed to passengers in 1955. The station was the starting point, in the 1950s and 1960s, of what may have been the smallest named train in the world, 'The Welsh Dragon'. This service ran from Llandudno to Rhyl and was usually made up of only two coaches and operated on a push-pull basis until replaced by DMU trains. Just before the scene in this photograph the Marine Lake is passed, with its miniature railway, and the estuary of the River Clwyd can be seen at Foryd, where the line to Denbigh trails in from the right. From here, the track runs close to the sea until the 'Irish Mail' reaches the outskirts of Bangor.

Author's collection

The castellated western portal of the Penmaenrhos Tunnel, 1960s. As a sign that the 'Irish Mail' is now in a resort area, caravan sites line the route between Rhyl and Abergele, the next station on the CHR. After leaving Abergele the 'Irish Mail' crosses the River Dulas on a short viaduct, and just beyond is Llandulas station which was destroyed by fire in 1913. A Down 'Irish Boat Express' was passing at the time, but only its coaches were scorched. Further west was Llysfaen station, where, in the early years of the twentieth century, a landslide blocked the railway at Llysfaen. It was spotted by a railway worker who, knowing a train was due, took off his red tie and waved it as a warning. He did not have time to clear the tracks before the train pulled up so he lay flat on the trackbed. After the train had stopped he crawled from underneath completely unhurt. After passing the site of Llysfaen the 'Irish Mail' enters the 487 yd Penmaenrhos Tunnel. Immediately afterwards the line crosses over the 1983 built Tan-y-Lan Viaduct which carries the railway above the A55 expressway as it reverts to the landward side.

D. Ibbotson

LNWR 'Greater Britain' 2–2–2–2 No. 2051 *George Findlay* at the head of a Chester-bound stopping train, Old Colwyn station, 1905. The site of Old Colwyn station is half a mile beyond Penmaenrhos Tunnel. The station opened in 1884, becoming Old Colwyn a year later after its original name of 'Colwyn' caused confusion with nearby Colwyn Bay station. Old Colwyn closed in May 1964.

Roger Carpenter collection

A little west of Old Colwyn the 'Irish Mail' enters Colwyn Bay station, seen here with a steam excursion to Holyhead, headed by preserved ex-LMS 'Princess Royal' Pacific No. 6201 *Princess Elizabeth*, 1989.

Author

At the site of Mochdre and Pabo station ex-LMS 'Jubilee' class 4–6–0 No. 45583 *Assam* is passing on a Down train, mid-1950s. Beyond Colwyn Bay station the track formation was realigned in 1983/4 and the new A55 expressway now occupies the old trackbed, running parallel with the railway as far as Llandudno Junction. The site of the old Mochdre and Pabo station, opened in 1889 and closed in the 1920s, is where the old track formation is regained. Mochdre was the site of the first water troughs anywhere in the world. Land to the extreme right of the station site is now part of the A55 expressway.

Gwyn Roberts

A local train leaving the original Llandudno Junction station, *c.* 1890. Approaching Llandudno Junction the 'Irish Mail' passes under a concrete bridge, carrying the new section of the A470 to Llandudno, and a stone bridge, which carries the old A55 road to Llandudno Junction. Curving away to the left is the Conwy Valley branch to the slate town of Blaenau Ffestiniog, opened as far as Llanrwst in 1863. To the right is the derelict Hotpoint washing-machine factory, just before the train passes under a three-arch bridge to enter Llandudno Junction station. The present station opened in 1897 and replaced the original 1860-built station that was situated a little further west. A station was built there to deal with extra traffic created when a branch to Llandudno was opened in 1858 and in preparation for the opening of the Conwy Valley Line.

Author's collection

LNWR 'Precedent' class 2–6–0 No. 1531 *Cromwell* rests at Llandudno Junction shed, *c.* 1920. In 1879 a locoshed with capacity for twelve engines was opened to the west of the present station, and in 1898 capacity was increased to twenty-four. Carriage sheds were constructed alongside, but burned down in the early 1990s, and in recent years the whole area has been used to service DMU sets. In November 1980 a new freight terminal, transferred from Colwyn Bay, began to operate on the site.

Author's collection

Ex-LNWR 2–4–2 tank No. 6666 heads a local service to Llandudno and rests at Llandudno Junction station, 1929.

Author's collection

An unidentified class 47 locomotive heads a Holyhead-bound express out of Llandudno Junction, 7 February 1988. In the background a railway ballast train from Penmaenmawr heads towards Warrington.

Gwyn Roberts

The complex of tracks west of Llandudno Junction, with the branch to Llandudno going off to the right, 1950s. At that time a level crossing marked the entrance to the branch and was a road-traffic bottleneck in the summer months, as was the suspension bridge at Conwy. A new road flyover solved the problem in the short term but Conwy itself was still the cause of traffic jams, which were only solved with the opening of the A55 expressway which avoided Conwy altogether. In the background an express, possibly the 'Irish Mail', can be seen approaching Llandudno Junction from Holyhead.

Clwyd Record Office

Looking back towards Llandudno Junction station, with Llandudno Junction No. 2 signal-box in view and the Llandudno branch curving away to the left, 1950s. On the right are the sidings to the Conwy riverside quay, and on the left, Fyffes banana warehouse, which is now an antiques shop.

Clwyd Record Office

An Up parcels train, headed by an LNWR 0–6–0 engine, leaves Robert Stephenson's tubular bridge as it heads towards Llandudno Junction, *c.* 1900. On leaving Llandudno Junction the 'Irish Mail' climbs up to the tubular bridge before entering Conwy. On the right is Thomas Telford's suspension bridge, built to cross the River Conwy as part of his Holyhead Road.

Author's collection

The railway and tubular bridge at Conwy, *c.* 1930. The tubular bridge was built as a prototype for the more ambitious Britannia Bridge, which crosses the Menai Strait into Anglesey, and has a span of 424 ft. The bridge portals were castellated to blend in with the nearby Conwy Castle, which can be seen on the left.

Author's collection

The eastern approach to the station at Conwy, then spelt 'Conway', *c.* 1890. The goods siding are nestling against the town wall around the castle. Here the 'Irish Mail' takes a sharp right-hand curve on its approach to the station and goes through a 'medieval' pointed stone arch, which pierced the town wall, to enter the station. The sidings were closed in 1964.

D. Ibbotson collection

Heading a ballast train from Penmaenmawr through the medieval arch at Conwy is a class 40 diesel on its way towards Llandudno Junction, mid-1970s.

Ron Watson-Jones

The eastern end of the Up platform of Conway (Conwy) station showing the medieval arch and main line curving away towards Llandudno Junction, c. 1900. The main building was designed by Francis Thompson and the station opened with the CHR in 1848. Before water troughs were opened at Mochdre the 'Irish Mail' always stopped at Conway to take on water, and the station assumed the important role of dealing with Llandudno trains until Llandudno Junction station was able to do this itself.

D. Ibbotson collection

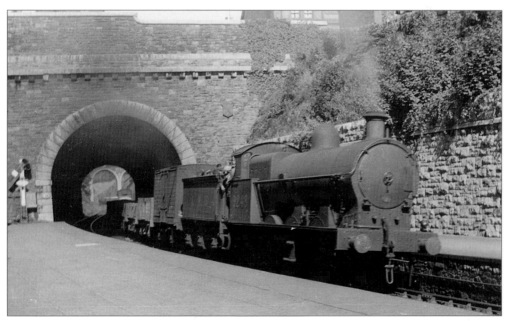

Ex-LNWR 7F 0–8–0 LMS No. 9248 enters Conway Station via the 74 yd Conway Tunnel as it heads an Up goods train, c. 1935. Conway station was closed in February 1966, although a new Conwy station, financed by Gwynedd County Council, was opened on 27 June 1987 as a means of relieving congestion caused by the construction of the A55 expressway.

Author's collection

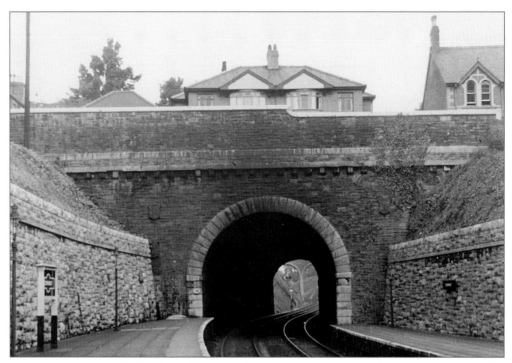

On leaving Conwy, the 'Irish Mail' enters the Conwy Tunnel, seen here in 1952 with the LMS 'Hawkseye' station nameboard visible on the left, as it heads towards Conwy Morfa. From this point the train travels through the foothills of Snowdonia all the way to the Britannia Bridge.

D. Ibbotson

The lone BR three-cylinder Pacific No. 71000 *Duke of Gloucester* heads a Down express towards Penmaen-bach Tunnel, 21 July 1962. After taking a left-hand curve and passing through a short cutting the 'Irish Mail' crosses above the old A55 road and passes the site of Conwy Morfa station. There were once military camps near here, which were served by the station until it closed in 1927. As the line heads towards Penmaen-bach Tunnel it is accompanied by the A55 expressway on the left.

Peter Owen

Ex-LMS class 5 4–6–0 No. 44913 at the head of an Up freight train having left the Penmaen-bach Tunnel and with the mountain of Penmaenmawr coming into view behind, *c.* 1965. Also in the background is the gas works site, cleared away as part of the A55 expressway development, and where even earlier there had been a school. In the early days of the railway boys at the school threw stones at passing trains, and this became such a problem that the school had to be closed and moved nearer to the town of Penmaenmawr.

Peter Owen

A 'Pacer' DMU set on an Up local train near Penmaenmawr, late 1980s. The green fields that adjoin the line to Penmaenmawr have now been taken over by the A55 expressway and the tunnel taking the new road through Penmaen-bach can be seen in the top left-hand corner. This photograph was taken from a bridge that crosses the line and leads to a youth hostel, which has now closed because sea erosion made it unsafe.

Gwyn Roberts

On the approach to Penmaenmawr station ex-LMS 'Jubilee' class 4–6–0 No. 45595 *Southern Rhodesia* heads an Up mail train, not the 'Irish Mail', east towards Llandudno Junction, *c.* 1960. On the right two young ladies are standing behind the sea wall watching the train go by, while, on the left, the first houses of Penmaenmawr are visible with the workings of the granite quarry behind. Penmaenmawr is encircled by mountains and it is an ideal holiday resort with its wide beaches and mountains. It is also sheltered from the rain and is one of the drier towns in Wales.

Gwyn Roberts

Class 40 diesel locomotive No. 40014 *Antonia* enters the eastern end of Penmaenmawr station with a container train for Holyhead. The train is passing the 1953 signal-box, which replaced the one that stood at the other end of the station. The siding entrance, seen here on the left, is obstructed by the station footbridge from the old signal-box, which was situated at the western end of the station, and this caused the accident here involving the 'Irish Mail' in 1950.

Ron Watson-Jones

Ex-LNWR 'Cauliflower' 0–6–0 No. 8485 at the head of a local train for Bangor coming to a halt at Penmaenmawr station, 23 August 1937. This station opened in November 1849, by which time the town was already established as a high-class holiday resort thanks to the patronage of Liberal statesman William Gladstone, who visited often as a guest of local quarry owner Charles Darbishire, also a Liberal. Evidence of the town's status as a retreat of the wealthy can be seen in the background – affluent visitors had smart houses constructed for them to stay in.

Roger Carpenter collection

With Penmaenmawr mountain brooding behind, a class 45 1Co–Co1 diesel-electric locomotive arrives at Penmaenmawr with an Up train, c. 1985. These engines became a common sight at Penmaenmawr on Trans-Pennine expresses and on ballast trains between 1983 and 1987. The station took its name from the mountain behind because the railway company felt that the parish name of Dwygyfylchi would be too complicated for passengers to pronounce, and Penmaenmawr was adopted as the town name soon afterwards too.

Ron Watson-Jones

The granite workings at Penmaenmawr, 1930s. Aside from being a holiday resort, Penmaenmawr is also a major granite-mining centre, stone being extracted from Penmaenmawr mountain. Quarrying began here in about 1830, but it was not until the LNWR placed an initial order for a million tons of railway ballast in 1888 that the quarry began producing such material, and it is still sent from Penmaenmawr every week. The LNWR were so impressed with Penmaenmawr granite that they used it on the whole of its railway network.

Author's collection

Class 47 locomotive No. 47555 *The Commonwealth Spirit* is hauling the Royal Train away from Penmaenmawr station, 11 July 1980. As well as their role as a loading area for stone products, Penmaenmawr sidings have also been used as a stabling point for the Royal Train. After an overnight stay HRH The Prince of Wales is travelling to the Britannia Bridge for a ceremony to reopen it officially after a fire had destroyed the original tubes.

Gwyn Roberts

An unidentified class 25 B-Bo locomotive heads away from Penmaenmawr towards Llanfairfechan with yet another ballast train, late 1970s. The extensive quarry sidings can be seen beyond. These were rationalised to make way for the A55 expressway which runs to the seaward side here and the construction of which swept away the town's original promenade, which was replaced by a new one, the first new promenade anywhere in Britain since Victorian times.

Ron Watson-Jones

Penmaenmawr Viaduct from the seaward side, c. 1900. From Penmaenmawr station and its quarry sidings the 'Irish Mail' heads towards Llanfairfechan, passes under a flyover that carries the A55 expressway back to the landward side and through a tunnel under Penmaenmawr mountain into Llanfairfechan. The 'Irish Mail also enters Penmaenmawr Tunnel, originally 254 yd long but with stone shelters added at each end to protect the line from rockfalls, and on to Penmaenmawr Viaduct, which has thirteen piers. When the CHR was originally built an embankment carried the line from the tunnel into Llanfairfechan but the sea kept washing it away, so the viaduct was built.

Author's collection

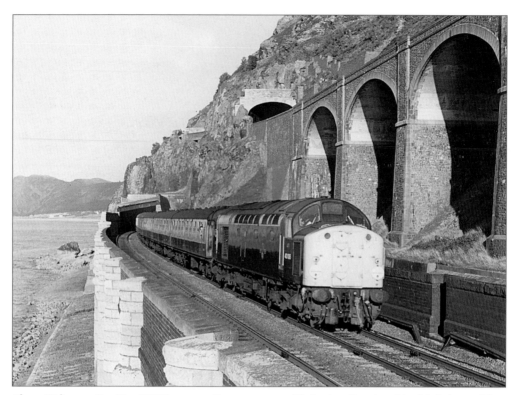

Class 40 locomotive No. 40106 crosses Penmaenmawr Viaduct as it enters Llanfairfechan with a Holyhead-bound train, 4 September 1979. The 1930s-built A55 road and tunnel can be seen on the right of the picture; this road now forms part of the eastbound A55 expressway.

Ron Watson-Jones

Ex-LNWR 'Precursor' class 4–4–0 No. 25277 runs through Llanfairfechan with a semi-fast train from Bangor, *c.* 1941. The workings of Penmaenmawr quarries can be seen in the background, along with Llanfairfechan school, chapel and the grand homes built for holiday-makers brought here by the railway.

Author's collection

Llanfairfechan station, looking towards Penmaenmawr, 1977. After rounding a curve the 'Irish Mail' enters Llanfairfechan station, which was opened in 1860 and turned the town into a booming tourist centre. Construction of the A55 expressway led to the 1860-built station being demolished in 1987, to be replaced with a new simple structure which was opened in 1989.

N. Mundy

The water troughs at Aber, some 2 miles west of Llanfairfechan, which were constructed to replace those at Mochdre, c. 1950. The troughs allowed the 'Irish Mail' to pick up water without stopping and therefore increased the speed of the train. In the background Penmaenmawr mountain is visible.

Roger Carpenter collection

The station at Aber with a train headed by an unidentified 4–4–0 arriving, *c.* 1900. Aber was the only station to open between Conwy and Bangor in 1848, but the area around remained rural. The station, however, survived until closure in 1960.

Author's collection

The 'Irish Mail' now moves slightly inland as it covers the 5½ miles between Aber and Bangor. An LMS 'Royal Scot' No. 6101 *Royal Scots Grey* traverses this section in about 1934, with the Bangor portion of *The Welshman* from Euston to resorts on the North Wales and Cambrian coasts, the train dividing at Prestatyn, one portion for Llandudno, and one for Bangor and then Afon Wen.

H.A. Coulter

Ex-LNWR 'Claughton' class 4–6–0 at the head of a train from Manchester at Penrhyn sidings, *c.* 1930. On its way to Bangor, and close to sidings that once existed at Tal-y-Bont for slate traffic from the quarries at nearby Bethesda.

H.A. Coulter

Bangor station No. 1 signal-box in the foreground, 1950s. Just before arriving in Bangor the 'Irish Mail' passes the trackbed, on the left, of the old Bethesda branch, which served this slate-quarrying town. The branch was closed to passengers in 1951 and to freight in 1963. The train then enters the 913 yd Bangor Tunnel, which has an Egyptian-style portico at the station end, and emerges into Bangor station where the two tracks fan out into four. Between 1848 and 1850, when the Britannia Bridge opened, Bangor was the terminus of the 'Irish Mail', and passengers were then transferred to road coaches operated by Mr Wright for the journey over the Menai suspension bridge to Llanfair PG where a train on the newly opened line to Holyhead was waiting. Once the bridge over the Menai Strait was opened, the road coaches became redundant.

Author's collection

Rebuilt 'Royal Scot' class 4–6–0 No. 46157 *The Royal Artilleryman* waits at Bangor station with a Down train for Holyhead, mid-1960s.

Gwyn Roberts

Bangor station looking east from Belmont Tunnel, showing the No. 2 signal-box and locoshed, 1930s. The 'Irish Mail' enters Belmont Tunnel and runs round a curve as it heads towards the site of Menai Bridge station.

Author's collection

Ex-LMS class 5 4–6–0 No. 44678 heads an Up train past Menai Bridge station, 29 August 1959.
A.G. Ellis collection

Menai Bridge station, *c.* 1953. The station was once a junction of the branch to Caernarfon and Afon Wen, where a connection was made with the Cambrian Railways route to Pwllheli and Barmouth. The section from Caernarfon to Afon Wen was closed in 1964, and Bangor to Caernarfon closed to freight in 1969 and to passengers in 1970. Caernarfon goods yard was reopened as a temporary container terminal in June 1970 following the Britannia Bridge fire, and finally closed in January 1972. Menai Bridge station closed to passengers in February 1966 but was reopened for cattle traffic and closed again at the same time as the Caernarfon goods yard.
Author's collection

Another ex-LNWR 'Prince of Wales' class 4–6–0 No. 5789 heads an Up cattle train from Holyhead through the portal of the Britannia Bridge. Shipment of cattle from Ireland was an important source of traffic for Holyhead and the railway companies.

H.A. Coulter

The new Britannia Bridge, rebuilt after the original tubes were destroyed by fire on 23 May 1970, seen here in 1971. However, this was not the first fire in the bridge tubes. On 13 July 1946 a painter's blow-lamp overturned inside the Up line tube at the Anglesey end and started a fire just as the 'Irish Mail' was passing through. Fortunately, the blaze was brought under control and the bridge was only closed for 5 hours. In 1970, however, the situation was much worse as the timber tube linings became fully ablaze because air currents fanned the flames. The wrought-iron tubes were subjected to such fierce heat that they sagged in the middle. As a result, all traffic was ceased and Down trains were terminated at Bangor, including the 'Irish Mail', and passengers had to continue their journey to Holyhead by road. Thus, Bangor took on its 1848–50 role as terminus of the 'Irish Mail' until the bridge was reconstructed. The new bridge, although it used the existing piers, abandoned the tubes in favour of an arched structure. The bridge remained closed until 30 January 1972, when an excursion DMU set from Chester to Holyhead passed over it on the newly relaid Up line. Work on the new bridge continued until 1975, although when complete the bridge remained single line only. The bridge was officially reopened by HRH The Prince of Wales on 11 July 1980 and was the reason why the Royal Train, see p. 106, had been stabled overnight in Penmaenmawr. After the bridge had been repaired the Welsh Office requested that a road bridge be constructed above the railway to relieve traffic congestion over the Menai suspension bridge. This work was undertaken between 1977 and 1980, and has led to the lions that have guarded the Britannia Bridge, and which were cared for while the new railway bridge was under reconstruction, being obscured by the approach to the new road deck. The 150th anniversary of the opening of the Britannia Bridge was celebrated on 18 March 2000 when a steam special excursion was run from Crewe.

Jim Roberts

Llanfair PG station, displaying its full name, 1930. The Britannia Bridge is crossed in a few seconds and on the left is a statue of Lord Nelson at the edge of the Menai Strait. It has long been used by shipping as a warning of rocks in the area. A sharp left curve follows after leaving the bridge before double track is resumed, just before a small overbridge. The 'Irish Mail' is now on the island of Anglesey (or Môn in Welsh). The first station on the island is Llanfair PG, which opened just in time to receive the first 'Irish Mail' passengers. The original wooden station burned down on 13 November 1865 and a replacement building was constructed in 1866. The station closed in 1964 but was reopened as a temporary structure, a short distance west, in May 1970. It was closed again in January 1972 only to be reopened in May 1973. The station buildings were sold to a Scottish woollen manufacturer in 1986 and have become a tourist attraction.

Author's collection

An unidentified class 47 diesel-electric locomotive passes through Llanfair PG with an express for Holyhead, late 1980s. The old Saxby and Farmer LNWR signal-box at the site of the original station can be seen on the left.

Gwyn Roberts

A local train from the Amlwch branch waits at Gearwen station en route to Bangor, 19 July 1963. After a long curve, some 2¾ miles on from Llanfair PG, the site of Gaerwen station is reached; it closed to passengers on 14 February 1966. Almost immediately afterwards the branch to Amlwch curves away to the left. Opened between 1864 and 1867 the branch closed to passengers in December 1964, but was used for many years for freight trains from the Associated Octel works at Amlwch. There have been some suggestions that the line could be preserved and a steam-train service operated over the route.

R.M. Casserley

The sidings at Gaerwen station with an ex-LNWR 0–6–2 tank locomotive, LMS No. 7596, being serviced in preparation for duty, 21 July 1934. After leaving Gaerwen the 'Irish Mail' heads through two tunnels at Bodorgan, the first of which is 413 yd long, while the second one is shorter. From Bodorgan the 'Irish Mail' will pass the station, followed by Ty Croes, Rhosneigr and Valley (where an RAF base is situated) before crossing a causeway that links Anglesey with Holy Island and entering the terminus at Holyhead.

H.C. Casserley

CHAPTER THREE

HOLYHEAD – THE TERMINUS OF THE 'IRISH MAIL'

A general view of the railway approach to Holyhead, showing the main line to the station, the locoshed with its complement of steam locomotives and the coaling stage, 1949. On the extreme left is the goods yard which once contained cattle pens and a cattle dock, the Irish beef trade being an important source of revenue for the port, station and railway company.

Peter Owen collection

Situated on the northern edge of Holy Island, a small isle just west of Anglesey and approached via a causeway built by Thomas Telford between 1815 and 1819 as part of his Holyhead Road, Holyhead has been an important terminus for trains connecting with boats for Ireland since 1848, although the town has been associated with Irish traffic for several centuries. The railway from Holyhead station is perhaps most famous for its 1 in 92 incline which has produced some spectacular pyrotechnics from famous old steam locomotives as they laboured away from Holyhead with heavy eastbound expresses to Euston, Liverpool and Manchester. The most famous train to terminate here is, of course, the 'Irish Mail'. Indeed, it was considered so important that the stationmaster always wore a buttonhole whenever this famous train arrived or departed.

Along with the well-known politicians and statesmen who have used the station to reach Ireland, many native Irish people have arrived at Holyhead as immigrants looking for work. They have also returned to Holyhead to take packet boats back to Ireland to visit relatives. Indeed, even today, for the same reason, expatriate Irish people and their descendants still use the 'Irish Mail' and other trains to connect with boats for Ireland. Another source of traffic at Holyhead has been the booming tourist industry in Ireland, many holiday-makers still using the port to sail across the Irish Sea. Sadly, the majority now come to Holyhead by car, although the railway and the 'Irish Mail' still have a role to play in the tourist trade.

To accommodate 'Irish Mail' and packet-boat passengers at Holyhead the CHR authorised the construction of a temporary station at a cost of £800 in March 1848. This temporary station was a rudimentary wooden structure, and was completed in July of that year. Captain Simmons, of the Board of Trade, considered the station incomplete and accommodation poor. Horse-drawn omnibuses operated between the station and Admiralty Pier, where 'Irish Mail' passengers waited in the open air to board packet boats to Ireland. Many passengers complained of the poor facilities at Holyhead, not least John Boothby, a recently resigned director of the CHR. He had become a director of the Great Southern & Western Railway in Ireland, and was, at that time, negotiating arrangements for Cork traffic to use Holyhead rather than the South Wales Railway's (later GWR) port at New Milford, Pembrokeshire. His major complaint was that there were no refreshment facilities for passengers arriving from Ireland who were forced to wait for connecting trains. Indeed, it was impossible to obtain any food or drinks until trains arrived in Chester. In response to this complaint more than any other an immediate order was given by the shamefaced CHR directors to spend £50 on extending the station waiting room so that refreshments could be provided.

BR 'Standard' class 5 4–6–0 No. 73053 arriving at Holyhead with the 10.31 a.m. train from Manchester Exchange, 14 August 1965. This was one of the many trains that ran to Holyhead in connection with boats for Ireland along with the 'Irish Mail'. The train is passing Holyhead locoshed with its allocation of locomotives, which included LMS class 5 4–6–0s and class 3F 0–6–0Ts, the latter used on station pilot and shunting duties at the port. Also in view is an unidentified BR 'Britannia' class Pacific which is being prepared to haul the Up 'Irish Mail' to Euston later in the day and a couple of DMU train sets used on local services between Anglesey and Bangor. A fitted freight train is also seen departing from Holyhead.

Peter Owen collection

BR English Electric Type 4 (class 40) 1Co–Co1 diesel-electric locomotive No. 40073 approaches Holyhead with a container train for Ireland, mid-1970s. After the demise of steam, these engines became a common sight on passenger and freight trains along the North Wales coast and at Holyhead, and were often in charge of the 'Irish Mail'.

Author's collection

Holyhead locoshed with its complement of the Euston company's locos, *c.* 1920. A 'Precursor' 4–4–0 can be seen in the background being prepared for express passenger duties and a Ramsbottom 0–6–0 'Special Tank' is in the foreground. These 'Special Tanks' were used to haul trains from Holyhead station to Admiralty Pier, where 'Irish Mail' passengers embarked on boats for Ireland until the early 1920s. As it was such an important terminus for Irish traffic, particularly the 'Irish Mail', Holyhead was provided with a locoshed by the CHR as soon as the station came into use. The initial shed measured 105 ft by 65 ft, but its size was increased threefold after complaints by Francis Trevithick, Locomotive Superintendent of the Northern Division of the LNWR, who supplied motive power for the CHR, that the facilities were totally inadequate. In those early days the shed was allocated a number of small tank engines for use on trains from Llanfair PG to Holyhead until the Britannia Bridge was opened in 1850. By the mid-1850s the shed was also allocated 2–2–2 locos *Cerberus* and *Pegasus*, which were for the exclusive use of 'Irish Mail' trains, and small tank engines for use on the Admiralty Pier line.

H.A. Coulter

Ex-LNWR Ramsbottom 'Special Tank' with LMS No. 27358 at Holyhead shed in the first year of the Grouping, 1923. By this time this locomotive was employed on shunting duties around the station. After takeover of the CHR by the LNWR a new shed was ordered, on the opposite side of the line to the original, in 1860. Opened a year later, it was built of stone with two pitched roofs and capacity for twelve engines. This new shed had four roads, a small coal stage and a 40 ft turntable. This table was later replaced with a 45 ft one and moved some distance down the shed yard to the south. The shed was coded 22 by the LNWR and its main function was to supply express engines for the 'Irish Mail'. The shed rarely had an allocation of more than twenty-five locos, the bulk being express types. Locomotives used on local trains across Anglesey to Holyhead were supplied by Bangor shed.

H.A. Coulter

Four locomotives at Holyhead shed, 3 August 1962. From left to right they are, LMS class 5 No. 45131, ex-LMS 'Duchess' Pacific No. 46239 *City of Chester* and class 5s nos 45380 and 45300. The 'Duchess' Pacifics were transferred to Holyhead from the West Coast Main Line in the early 1960s following modernisation and were to be seen on the North Wales coast until withdrawal in 1965. In 1935 the shed was supplied with wheeldrop facilities, a new coaling plant and a 70 ft turntable. A new 'Louvre'-pattern LMS-style roof was fitted to the shed in 1950.

Peter Owen collection

A pair of class 5s, nos 45247 and 44821, and an unidentified class 40 diesel-electric loco at Holyhead shed, mid-1960s. These class 40 locomotives were allocated to Holyhead to work the 'Irish Mail' from 1963, and oil tanks with refuelling facilities were provided in the shed yard at the same time. Steam traction, however, remained at Holyhead until 1966, the last steam allocation being twelve class 5s.

Author's collection

In BR green livery English Electric Type 4 (later class 40) No. D288 is in the company of an LMS class 3F 0–6–0T at Holyhead shed, 30 July 1963. The shed was closed on 12 December 1966, but it survived intact, housing DMU sets, 'Sprinter' and 'Pacer' units that operated local services between Holyhead, Bangor and Llandudno Junction, along with class 08 diesel shunters and the occasional class 47 diesel-electric locomotive, until it was finally demolished in 1989. Examples of the shed allocations are given below.
Author's collection

Holyhead Locoshed Allocations
Codes:
LNWR – 22; LMS – 7C; BR – 6J

February 1946

Stanier class 5 4–6–0	5110,* 5112, 5113, 5249, 5313
'Royal Scot' 4–6–0	6112 *Sherwood Forester*, 6127 *The Old Contemptible*, 6145 *The Duke of Wellington's Regt. (West Riding)*
LNWR 0–6–2 'Coal Tank'	6899
LMS class 3F 0–6–0T	7321, 7368, 7476
Total: 12	

November 1950

Stanier class 5 4–6–0	44864, 44865, 44868, 45070, 45110*, 45111, 45249, 45346, 45382
'Royal Scot' 4–6–0	46112 *Sherwood Forester*, 46119 *Lancashire Fusilier*, 46127 *The Old Contemptible*, 46130 *The West Yorkshire Regiment*, 46132 *The King's Regiment (Liverpool)*, 46161 *King's Own*, 46166 *London Rifle Brigade*
LMS class 3F 0–6–0T	47321, 47368, 47476
Total: 19	

March 1954

Stanier class 5 4–6–0	44678, 44681, 44864, 44865, 44868, 45045, 45110,* 45292, 45382
LMS 'Compound' 4–4–0	41115
'Royal Scot' 4–6–0	46110 *Grenadier Guardsman*, 46127 *The Old Contemptible*, 46129 *The Scottish Horse*, 46132 *The King's Regiment (Liverpool)*, 46150 *The Life Guardsman*, 46157 *The Royal Artilleryman*
LMS class 3F 0–6–0T	47321, 47368, 47476
Total: 19	

* 45110 has been preserved, and is part of the collection of the Severn Valley Railway, where the locomotive is known as *RAF Biggin Hill*.

June 1963

Stanier class 5 4–6–0	44807, 44865, 45110
'Patriot' class 4–6–0	45527 *Southport*
'Jubilee' class 4–6–0	45736 *Phoenix*
'Royal Scot' class 4–6–0	46114 *Coldstream Guardsman*, 46125 *3rd Carabinier*, 46148 *The Manchester Regiment*, 46150 *The Life Guardsman*, 46152 *The King's Dragoon Guardsman*, 46156 *The South Wales Borderer*, 46167 *The Hertfordshire Regiment*
LMS class 3F 0–6–0T	47321, 47368, 47439, 47476
BR 'Britannia' 4–6–2	70026 *Polar Star*, 70027 *Rising Star*, 70045 *Lord Rowallan*, 70046 *Anzac*
Total: 20	

December 1966 (Last Allocation)

Stanier class 5 4–6–0	44770, 44771, 44807, 44831, 44866, 45001, 45043, 45048, 45116, 45247, 45280, 45405
Total: 12	

This drawing details the development of Holyhead station, showing the original station in 1850 and extensions undertaken by 1854. In 1851 plans were drawn up for an extension railway to Admiralty Pier, where 'Irish Mail' passengers boarded CDSPC 'Irish Mail' boats, which would replace road coaches then in use. In November 1850 the CHR noted that Moreton Peto, the CHR director, was in discussion with the Commissioners of Woods and Forests, who owned the land between the station and pier. In the event the Commissioners appointed James Rendel, who had been involved in work at Admiralty Pier, to take care of their interests in matters connected with the extension line. In December 1850 authorisation was given for construction of the extension line and orders were given that it should be ready in time for the opening of the Great Exhibition in 1851. The cost was estimated at £28,000 and the contract was awarded to George Giles. Early in 1850 it was decided that a new permanent station should be built, with improved refreshment facilities. The extension line carried its first passengers on Tuesday 20 May 1851, although it was actually scheduled to open on 15 May. The new extension line was not a success as it had so many tight curves and four horses were required to haul the, then, small coaches at a speed of 4 mph. Construction of the new station involved making a cutting a third of a mile long, and between 10 and 15 ft deep, the demolition of some ten houses, and filling and levelling of ground to make room for the station. A half-mile timber viaduct, with wooden drawbridge, was built alongside the harbour cliffs on which the horse-drawn railway carriages were carried to Salt Island. The wooden drawbridge was replaced with an iron structure in 1881.

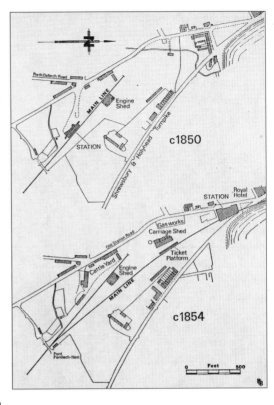

Author's collection

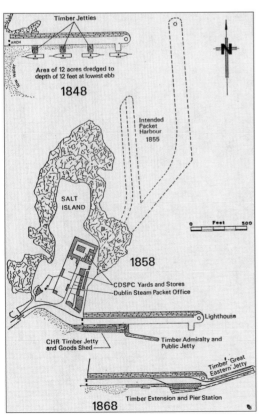

A plan showing the development of Admiralty Pier over twenty years from 1848. To operate trains over the extension steam locomotives had to travel at about 8 mph. Initially the LNWR provided two ex-Liverpool & Manchester Railway locos which had been converted to tank engines, but these did not last long as they were already worn out. By 1863 drawings were produced for small engines, and in December 1863 five 0–4–0 saddle tanks with 4 ft diameter wheels were completed at Crewe, with a further one added in January 1864. An extensive breakwater system was planned at Admiralty Pier, with a north breakwater of 5,360 ft and east breakwater of 1,570 ft with a packet pier, this and the east breakwater providing 3,000 ft of quay space. The packet pier was abandoned in 1855 when it was found that the north breakwater was of insufficient length. A timber extension was added to the pier in 1868. The trains that ran along the extension line were a source of delight and danger for local children, not least because passengers would often throw money out to them as they ran alongside the trains. In August 1852 a child was run over by a train on the extension line, but it was not until June 1855 that attempts were made to stop passengers throwing money through carriage windows. The police were also ordered to keep children away from the railway. In November 1857 strengthening work was carried out in order to allow the running of steam trains along the extension line, after the Board of Trade had given permission. In August 1859 Captain Ross inspected the line, and apart from work to a single-span bridge, extra fencing and the introduction of new signalling, allowed steam engines to work the line.

Author's collection

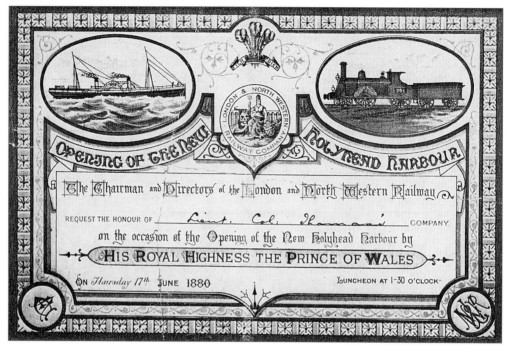

An invitation to the opening of the new Holyhead station and harbour works by the Prince of Wales, later Edward VII, on Thursday 17 June 1880. Holyhead station, designed by Charles Reed, was opened on 14 September 1851 and was situated near the junction of the Shrewsbury turnpike road and the old station road. It cost £2,800 and was described by the LNWR, in 1853, as being 'extensive and commodious in which were situated refreshment rooms, with waiting and dressing rooms attached; a telegraph office and well furnished book room'. Having failed to take the mail contract from the CDSPC, the LNWR planned new works at Holyhead, which included a new inner harbour and station. This work was to last for some twenty years. The new station and combined five-storey red-brick hotel was built as a fitting terminus for LNWR Irish services. Plans were agreed in April 1876, but the contract was not placed until 14 November 1877, when it went to J. Parnell & Son at a contract price of £64,807. With the opening of the new station and harbour, railway development at Holyhead was virtually complete, with the exception of essential alterations to keep the station up to date.

Author's collection

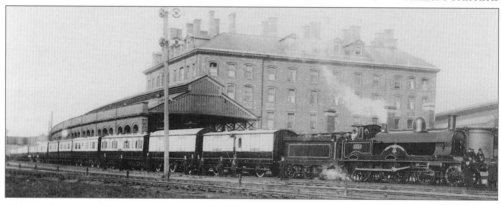

The royal train is about to depart from Holyhead behind LNWR 'Jubilee' class 4–4–0 Compound locomotive No. 1915 *Implacable*, 20 March 1900. The station, with hotel above, is seen in the background and had an elevation of 135 ft, side walls of 96½ ft and passenger quays to the east and west that were 550 ft long and 35 ft wide, with berth space for two vessels at each quay. This allowed direct transfer of passengers between train and ship. The main town frontage was provided with a covered porch and rear circulating area for passengers, with veranda.

Author's collection

The east quay at Holyhead station with passengers disembarking from LNWR packet boat *Anglia*, c. 1905. The hotel is visible on the extreme right with the station roof connected to it.

National Railway Museum

The inner harbour viewed from the station hotel with LNWR boat *Anglia* on the east quay (arrival) and *Galtee Moor* on the west (departure) quay, September 1905. In the background is the 150 ft by 54 ft warehouse that was constructed, along with a goods shed, in 1875. With the completion of these works the sidings accommodation covered 15 miles, and the total railway land at Holyhead extended over an area of 43 acres, 23 of which were reclaimed from water and wasteland. Trains were controlled from four signal-boxes, containing a total of 225 levers. These works were designed to cope with daily passenger traffic of about 1,000 people, 7 goods trains in and out per day, 149,000 sheep, 127,000 pigs, 54,500 cattle and 4,800 horses per year. Livestock had their own roads, bridges and inclined ways to move them to and from the import shed.

National Railway Museum

The east platform at Holyhead station with a train waiting to take packet-boat passengers on to Euston, 1905. It is likely that a boat has just arrived and among the finely attired passengers who have disembarked are a less well-dressed couple who perhaps have come to Great Britain from Ireland in the hope of making their fortune. The station platforms at the new station were 1,130 ft and 1,260 ft long on the east and west sides, respectively, connected directly with the quays and

were covered with a 'Euston'-style overall roof. Arrivals used the east quay, as can be seen in this photograph, and departures left from the west quay. The east quay also dealt with exports, while the west quay dealt with imported cattle and goods.

National Railway Museum

The main arrival platform at Holyhead (No. 3), *c.* 1960. On 30 August 1906 the GWR opened a new Irish packet port at Fishguard, Pembrokeshire, which gave the Paddington company the shortest sea crossing to Ireland (54 miles, compared to the 60 mile route from Holyhead), although the port of Rosslare was further away from Dublin. However, the GWR did take some traffic from the LNWR. In response in July 1906 the Euston company opened a new platform at Holyhead which had a moveable gangway connecting the east departure platform which allowed luggage to be transported between platforms more rapidly. They also began publicising the Holyhead route to Ireland more extensively. The moves were successful and Holyhead remained the chief port for Irish traffic.

Author's collection

Arrivals platform No. 3 from under the overall roof, 1960. In the background an LMS class 3F 0–6–0 tank locomotive is shunting wagons in the yard, while mail is being unloaded from the van at the front of the train on to the platform, possibly the 'Irish Mail' that arrived earlier in the day.

Author's collection

Departure platforms, No. 1 on the right and No. 2 on the left, covered by the rather dilapidated overall roof, c. 1960.

Author's collection

Departure platform No. 2, looking towards Bangor, 1960. A train is being prepared for departure and awaits a locomotive. In October 1999 Holyhead station was the scene of a near miss when a Down Virgin Trains IC125 from Euston was routed on to the same track as a departing Sprinter train for Manchester. The driver of the Euston train braked in time to prevent a collision. This occurred at a time when questions were being asked about railway safety following the Paddington disaster.

Author's collection

Following her visit to the USA, *The Royal Scot* is on display at Holyhead, 1934. She has a bell fitted to the buffer beam and a headlamp above the smokebox in the American style. It was fitting that the locomotive was displayed here, given that this class of engine featured so prominently in the history of the 'Irish Mail', which can be seen alongside. A good crowd has gathered to admire the engine.

Author's collection

The arrival side at Holyhead with LMS Caprotti valve-geared class 5 460 No. 44749 of Longsight (9A) shed, Manchester, at the head of a fitted freight train, 19 August 1956.

Peter Owen collection

Ex-Southern Railway 'Merchant Navy' class Pacific No. 35028 *Clan Line* at Holyhead at the head of the 'North Wales Coast Express', 1989. This service ran throughout the summer of 1989. Although steam traction finished at Holyhead in 1966, the railway between Crewe and Holyhead was allowed to operate preserved steam locomotives, the first being No. 35028 on 14 February 1989.

Brenda Roberts

Another steam excursion along the North Wales coast, this time, the 'Ynys Môn Express' with ex-LMS 'Princess Royal' class Pacific No. 46203 *Princess Margaret Rose* in charge, 12 October 1991. Rail traffic to Holyhead had been in decline since the 1960s in favour of road transport and these changes brought about the redevelopment of the station in 1978. The Station Hotel was demolished in that year to create an all-year-round car-ferry operation, with a new terminal, seen in the right background, being built on the site. Also, improvements were made to the customs hall, baggage and mail facilities. The station itself was modernised with a new booking office, waiting rooms and a small buffet. The old 'Euston'-style overall roof was removed and replaced with canopies over the platforms.

Brenda Roberts

A portrait of No. 46203 *Princess Margaret Rose* at the head of the 'Ynys Môn Express', 12 October 1991. This is a reminder of when locomotives of this class were in charge of the 'Irish Mail' in the 1940s while the 'Royal Scots' were being reboilered.

Gwyn Roberts

Ex-LMS 'Princess Royal' class Pacific No. 46203 *Princess Margaret Rose* being turned on the triangle at Valley, just outside Holyhead, before heading tender first back to Holyhead to take her train back to Crewe, 16 January 1994. With the locoshed at Holyhead having closed in the mid-1960s, there were no facilities to turn steam engines so a triangle was put in at Valley for this purpose when the CHR began operating steam excursions. It is also used as a storage area for nuclear flask trains from the nearby Wylfa nuclear power station.

Brenda Roberts

A preserved class 40, another locomotive type that once hauled the 'Irish Mail', is seen at the head of an excursion back to Crewe, 1980s. An unidentified class 47 with a rake of coaches is on the left and the overall roof is still in place above the arrivals platform, on the right, although it was removed shortly after this photograph was taken in preparation for the building of the new terminal.

Brenda Roberts

The Station Hotel, built as part of the 1880 station complex, 1890s. This hotel replaced the earlier one, the Eagle and Child Inn, from where stagecoaches to Euston departed. The LNWR bought the Eagle and Child in 1851 at a cost of £6,852, and after the LNWR had fitted it out it was described as a place of some elegance. All food was provided by Mrs Leonora Hibbert, who had become famous for the quality of her catering at Wolverton. Her relocation to Holyhead was considered by many to be a demotion, but she saw it as a promotion and considered that she had been brought especially to Holyhead at the behest of the LNWR and CHR to impress the large number of influential passengers who came through the station on their way to the Great Exhibition at the Crystal Palace. Mrs Hibbert agreed to the move in May 1851, and the LNWR took over the Eagle and Child and renamed it the Royal Hotel. Mrs Hibbert also managed the catering at the new station when it opened in 1851.

Jim Roberts

The Station Hotel, 1920s. The hansom cabs of the previous picture have been replaced by motor cars, the advent of which had a detrimental effect on the 'Irish Mail' train service and Holyhead station itself in the years after the Second World War.

Jim Roberts

The rear of the Station Hotel as it looked from the harbour, *c.* 1900. As the GWR began to compete for Irish traffic through its port at Fishguard, the LNWR began advertising the benefits of the climate at Holyhead and also produced a guide to the 65-bedroom Station Hotel, which ensured that Holyhead remained pre-eminent as the port for Irish traffic.

Jim Roberts

The Station Hotel from Holyhead harbour, *c.* 1900. The hotel survived until closure in 1951, and remained unused until it was demolished in 1978 to make way for a new car-ferry terminal.

Jim Roberts

The harbour, station and hotel at Holyhead from the air, *c.* 1920. In the background is Salt Island and the Admiralty Pier, with two steam packets of the LMS, who were still responsible for 'Irish Mail' traffic at the time. Also in view are the warehouses built in 1875. In October 1859 I.K. Brunel's iron steamship, the *Great Eastern*, was a visitor to Holyhead to see whether the, then, new harbour was suitable as a port of departure for her first transatlantic crossing, such was the importance of Holyhead at that time. There was great interest in the *Great Eastern*'s visit, and a banquet, attended by William Gladstone, then Chancellor of the Exchequer, and the railway and steamship directors, was held at the Station Hotel. The Royal family was also at Holyhead, and Prince Albert showed the French Prince Napoleon over the vessel. So much public interest was engendered by the great ship's visit that fifteen excursion trains arrived in Holyhead station in just one day. It was found, however, that the *Great Eastern* was too large for the port, with too little sea room for comfort. A great storm, which caused substantial damage on Anglesey and wrecked the *Royal Charter* off Moelfre with great loss of life, on the night of 24 and 25 October forced the *Great Eastern* to battle through the night to save herself from being swept ashore, and as soon as possible afterwards she left for Southampton, never to return to Holyhead again.

Jim Roberts

Warehouse and goods facilities at Holyhead, with the town in view on the other side of the harbour, *c.* 1900. The harbour, railway company and steam-packet operators were an important source of employment in the town and work could be found in the port, either dealing with passenger and freight traffic or as locomen, shed fitters, ship fitters or sailors. The decline of the port in recent years has led to the loss of many of these sources of employment, and Holyhead has become one of the most economically depressed towns in North Wales.

Jim Roberts

This LMS advertisement gives Holyhead
the accolade of 'holding the sunshine
record of Great Britain' and points out that
Holyhead is served by its mail route,
1930s. From 1906, when the LNWR
advertised the 'delights' of Holyhead, as
competition from the GWR was having its
effect, the railway companies continued to
promote the town as a resort area. The
drawing is of South Stack lighthouse,
which has long attracted visitors and still
does.

Author's collection

Holyhead harbour, looking towards Admiralty Pier, September 1905. The Admiralty Arch can be
seen in the background which marks the start of the A5 road and is smaller than Admiralty Arch
in London, where the A5 ends. A train can be seen on Admiralty Pier, from where mail boats
belonging to the CDSPC left for Kingstown (Dun Laoghaire). On the right, cargo vessels are being
unloaded. Sadly much freight has disappeared from Holyhead, and even container traffic, a feature
of the port from 1968, was discontinued in 1990. However, as the Channel Tunnel has since
opened and Holyhead has been classified as part of the Euro route to the tunnel, pressure has been
brought to bear to reinstate container traffic at the port, so far without success.

National Railway Museum

CHAPTER FOUR

'IRISH MAIL' PACKET BOATS

Sailing packet boats at the Admiralty Pier, Holyhead, eighteenth century. When the Chester & Holyhead Railway opened in 1848 the Admiralty were responsible for the carriage of mails across the Irish Sea. They took mailbags from the 'Irish Mail' train, which arrived in Holyhead at 7.05 a.m., and put them on the new paddle steamer Banshee to Kingstown, which arrived at 11.30 a.m. Three other boats, the Caradoc, Llewelyn and St Columba, were also used, but these were slower and took up to 5½ hours to make the journey between Holyhead and Kingstown.

Jim Robert

To continue the journey from London to Dublin 'Irish Mail' passengers have to cross the Irish Sea on packet boats to Dun Laoghaire, 7 miles from Dublin. Holyhead has long been an important port for sea transit to Ireland and mail packet services, directly licensed and controlled by the British Government, have operated between Holyhead and Dublin since the seventeenth century, when the journey took six days. All craft at Holyhead harbour were strictly supervised, and any boats that attempted to evade this control, by sailing round Anglesey to Beaumaris (on the southern side of the island), were followed and their crews seized. Troops were nearly always stationed at Holyhead to watch packet boats and to seize traitors and treacherous correspondence. The principal fear, in those days, was the papist influence in Ireland, and how this might lead to a Catholic insurrection in England, which was considered a serious threat to the Crown. When William of Orange became King in 1688 the subjugation of Ireland was completed, and regular military patrols around Anglesey and Holyhead did much to prevent illicit boat traffic reaching the British mainland.

During the seventeenth century regular passage to Ireland from Holyhead was undertaken by seven sailing packets which were based at the port. By 1819 new sea power was introduced when two steamers, the *Ivanhoe* and *Talbot* of the New Steam Packet Company, began operating between Holyhead and Ireland. At that time the main Irish port for Dublin was at Howth, but the harbour there had begun to silt up and by 1834 it was decided that the new, and as yet, incomplete, harbour at Dun Laoghaire, known as Kingstown after George IV had visited there in 1821, was to be the port for Irish mail traffic. This new harbour was completed in 1836. Following Irish independence, in 1922, the name Dun Laoghaire was revived.

The Post Office operated mails using their own steamers, *Lightning* of 205 tons and *Meteor* of 189 tons, from 1821. So successful were these boats that the New Steam Packet Company was forced to withdraw its ships from Holyhead. The PO ship *Lightning* carried King George IV to Ireland on 7 August 1821 after the Royal Yacht had been forced back to port owing to bad weather, and was re-christened *Royal Sovereign King George the Fourth* to commemorate the event. In 1822 *Lightning* (*Royal Sovereign*) made 143 crossings between Holyhead and Howth in an average time of 7 hours 39 minutes. In the same year the last mail crossing by sailing packets were undertaken. The final three boats, *Pelham*, *Montrose* and *Countess of Liverpool* spent several years afterwards as colliers supplying the steamers.

Steam ships operated by the City of Dublin Steam Packet Company were running from Liverpool to Dublin, calling at Holyhead on the way. These ships drastically affected Post Office passenger revenue. In the years from 1826, when competition was at its most intense, the Post Office boats cost £231,000 to run but receipts were only £140,000. By the time mails were being carried by rail to Liverpool the CDSPC had a virtual monopoly on sailings to Dublin and thus carried the mail in their own boats. While the Admiralty was responsible for carrying mails from the 'Irish Mail' train when the CHR opened in 1848, it was the CDSPC who won the contract for carriage of mail from 1850 until 1920.

An advertisement for the City of Dublin Steam Packet Company, showing the company's boat RMS *Munster* and emphasising the company's role as carrier of the mails to and from Ireland, *c.* 1900. The Admiralty ceased to be responsible for the mails from 1850, when the CDSPC won the contract for this traffic. The LNWR failed to tender, believing that as they already operated the 'Irish Mail' train they should have the contract by right; they did not obtain the contract to carry the mail until 1920. Mail packet boats always docked at Admiralty Pier, some 9 furlongs away from the railway station, and this was served by a horse-drawn tramway, known as the 'Irish Mail Line', later to be operated by small 0–4–0 saddle tank locomotives. LNWR 'Special Tanks' worked the trains to Admiralty Pier in the early years of the twentieth century.

Jim Roberts

After winning the mail contract, the CDSPC immediately put its boats on the Holyhead–Kingstown route in competition with those of the CHR/LNWR. One of that company's paddle steamers, the *Leinster*, is seen leaving Holyhead with the mails, *c.* 1880. These paddle steamers were introduced on the mail run in 1860 and, as well as the *Leinster*, three other boats were used, the *Munster*, *Connaught* and *Ulster*. These boats had a gross registered tonnage of 2,000 tons and had a speed of 15 knots. On 20 June 1861 the Prince of Wales crossed the Irish Sea on the *Connaught* in a time of 3 hours 38 minutes, a record at the time. The paddle steamer *Ireland* was added to the fleet in 1883. She was the fastest paddle steamer then built and capable of reaching a speed of 21 knots.

Jim Roberts

An LMS boat entering the inner harbour with the 'Irish Mail' service, *c.* 1920. The Admiralty Pier had been built in 1824 and the arch seen in this view was built to commemorate the visit of King George IV to Ireland in 1821. The CDSPC introduced the second *Ulster*, *Munster*, *Leinster* and *Connaught* in 1897. These new boats were screw driven, had a gross registered tonnage of 3,000 tons, had 9,000 hp and were capable of achieving 24 knots. They remained in service until after the First World War, with the exception of *Leinster*, which was torpedoed off the Kish lightship in 1915.

Jim Roberts

The *Cambria*, operated by the CHR, 1848. In 1848 the CHR purchased four paddle steamers, the *Anglia*, *Scotia*, *Hibernia* and *Cambria* to operate the mail service, believing that this would automatically ensure that they won the mail contract, but they were unsuccessful. The *Cambria* arrived in Holyhead the day before the inaugural 'Irish Mail' train, along with Admiralty boat *Banshee*, the former to take passengers across the Irish Sea, while the latter was to transport the mails.

Jim Roberts

An LNWR advertisement showing one of their boats passing the Kish lightship just off the Irish coast, *c.* 1910. Although the LNWR failed to take the mail contract, the company operated its own boats across the Irish Sea to Dublin, and advertised its services. From 1 May 1897 third-class passengers were carried on the 'Irish Mail' train and encouraged to use CDSPC boats in an attempt to leave the LNWR boats free for first- and second-class passengers. CHR/LNWR boats had been carrying third-class passengers since 1853 when that company withdrew through bookings via the CDSPC, and then the 'poorer classes', such as Irish labourers and harvestmen, increasingly used railway company boats to Ireland after coming to Holyhead on 'parliamentary trains'. The 'upper classes', who were aware of this, preferred to use the 'elegant' CDSPC boats and travelled on the 'Irish Mail'. As a result LNWR boat receipts fell and through booking was revived from January 1855.

National Railway Museum

The LNWR inner harbour with ex-LNWR packet boat *Cambria* on the right, *c.* 1921. In 1883 the mail contract came up for renewal and the LNWR tendered for it and secured it. Unfortunately for them, this caused a major political controversy and, at the request of government, the LNWR withdrew its tender and the contract reverted to the CDSPC. When the contract came up for renewal in 1897, it again went to the Dublin company in deference to Irish feelings, and they continued to hold it until 1920. However, during this time, packet boats increased in size and Admiralty Pier at Holyhead needed to be extended. In 1857 plans were drawn up for a new packet harbour on the eastern side of Salt Island close to the pier, with an estimated cost of £445,000. These plans were abandoned as they were considered too expensive, and just the pier was extended instead. Both the LNWR and CDSPC were unhappy with the first timber extension, arguing that it was inadequate to hold vessels during heavy storms. As if to prove this point, the CDSPC boat *Llewelyn* was nearly torn from its moorings by heavy storms on 27 May 1860. The LNWR decided that it would improve its own amenities at the station and build a new inner harbour that would provide good facilities for both trains and ships. This work was completed in 1880 and it was hoped it would help the LNWR win the mail contract. However, the new inner harbour was beset by silting problems which could sometimes ground ships and from 1902 a dredger was permanently stationed at Holyhead to combat this difficulty.

Jim Roberts

An LNWR packet boat in the inner harbour at Holyhead, *c.* 1920. The LNWR finally won the mail contract from the CDSPC on 28 November 1920, the *Curraghmore* bringing the first mails carried by the railway company from Ireland into Holyhead at 11.45 a.m. on Sunday 19 November. A second boat, the *Anglia*, arrived at 11.45 p.m. on the same day. All CDSPC staff at Holyhead were taken on by the LNWR from Monday 30 November 1920. Admiralty Pier continued to be used by the LNWR until March 1925 because new packet boats built to operate the mail contract could not use the inner harbour at Holyhead station until it had been sufficiently dredged to accommodate them. Boats operated from the inner harbour from 8 March 1925, and Admiralty Pier station closed on 1 April.

Jim Roberts

The inner harbour at Holyhead with one LNWR packet boat in view, *c.* 1910. By the time mail boats operated out of the inner harbour the LNWR had become part of the new London Midland & Scottish Railway following the 1923 Grouping, and all mail and packet boats were taken over by the LMS.

Jim Roberts

Admiralty Pier, Holyhead, with a CDSPC vessel alongside, *c.* 1910.

Author's collection

LNWR boat *Hibernia* leaving the inner harbour at Holyhead with passengers for Dublin, *c.* 1910.

Jim Roberts

LNWR packet boat *Connemara* departing from Holyhead, *c.* 1910. Not only did the railway company operate boats between Holyhead and Dublin, but they also ran freight and passenger services to Greenore and connections to Belfast from Holyhead.

Jim Roberts

One of the LNWR steamers refurbished by the LMS, 1939. After 'Irish Mail' services came under the control of the LMS in 1923, the new railway company refurbished three twin-screw steamers in the early 1930s, the *Cambria*, *Hibernia* and *Scotia*, all of which had been in service with the LNWR. These boats each had a gross registered tonnage of 3,400 tons with turbine engines capable of speeds up to 25 knots. These were among the fastest merchant ships anywhere in the world at this time.

Jim Roberts

The LMS mail boat *Hibernia* departing from Holyhead just before the outbreak of the Second World War.

Jim Roberts

LMS mail boat *Cambria* approaching Holyhead, 1938. The *Cambria* was bombed and strafed by a German aircraft as she crossed the Irish Sea on 19 December 1940. The Third Officer was fatally wounded and several bullets hit the vessel, causing some damage. This was the only time that 'Irish Mail' ships were attacked as they crossed the Irish Sea during the Second World War.

National Railway Museum

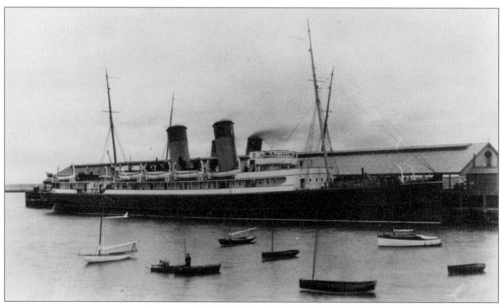

The LMS mail boat *Scotia* at Dun Laoghaire, 1920s. *Scotia* was one of the 'little ships' that were sent to Dunkirk to evacuate British troops. Sadly, *Scotia* was sunk as she tried to make the evacuation at Dunkirk, with great loss of life.

Jim Roberts

The *Cambria*, late 1950s. After the Second World War the LMS ordered two new 4,972 ton, diesel-powered ships on the Holyhead–Dun Laoghaire route, the *Cambria* and the *Hibernia*, which were completed and put into service by BR in 1949. They were ordinary passenger-ferry types, with separate first- and third-class facilities. Increasing car ownership in the post-war boom years and carriage of mail by air to Ireland meant that ships used on the Holyhead–Dun Laoghaire route became car and passenger ferries. The first, introduced in 1965, was *Holyhead Ferry I* and could carry 150 cars and 1,000 passengers. She was replaced in 1972 by the *Duke of Rothesay*. From 2 May 1977 a new 8,000 ton roll on/roll off ship, the *St Columba*, took over the Holyhead–Dun Laoghaire service, assisted in the summer by the 5,412 ton *Avalon*. By 1981 another vessel, the £16 million, 8,200 ton *St David*, came on station on 10 August. As she was delivered late, the 5,793 ton *Princess Desiree* was hired from Stena Lines to cover the 1981 summer season. By 1979 ferry services in the UK had adopted a separate identity from British Rail, becoming known as Sealink. In 1989 Sealink was privatised and in 1990 became Stena Sealink after merging with Swedish ferry company Stena Lines. In 1990 *St Columba* was taken out of service to be refurbished and returned as *Stena Hibernia* in 1991. A new ship, *Stena Cambria*, was introduced to Holyhead in 1991, both these names recalling old LNWR/LMS packet boats.

Jim Roberts

Today the Holyhead–Dun Laoghaire service is in the hands of fast, modern ships, epitomised by the Norwegian-built, twin-hulled HSS *Stena Explorer*, seen here at Holyhead in April 1999. The new vessel cost £65 million and can travel at twice the speed of a traditional ferry thanks to its four jet engines which produce 100,000 horsepower. The 126 m long and 40 m wide ship was scheduled to enter service in March 1996, but was damaged while undertaking trials and its delivery was delayed. The ship is now fully in service and offers a 99 minute trip across the Irish Sea. The arrival of this 'superferry' should ensure that Holyhead remains the most important port for Ireland.

Marian Forrest

Dun Laoghaire harbour, viewed from the HSS *Stena Explorer*, April 1999. On arrival at Dun Laoghaire it is a journey of 7 miles to Dublin, and this final leg of the journey can be completed by rail.

Marian Forrest

CHAPTER FIVE

THE IRISH CONNECTION

The station at Dun Laoghaire, Carlisle Pier, with a mail boat in the harbour, either the Sealink boat Cambria or Hibernia, 1970. The Railways (Conveyance of Mails) Act of 1838 brought a rapid increase in the transit of mails by rail. The volume of mail arriving at Kingstown from first Liverpool and then Holyhead could not easily be accommodated in passenger coaches, so the D&K converted some of its third-class carriages into vans, the first Irish railway mail vehicles. Charge for the mail service was calculated on the number of seats occupied by mailbags, until special vans were built, and were rounded off into the annual charge, at first £300, but raised to £500 when local mails were included. Mail boats arrived in Kingstown at 5.30 a.m., and mails were transferred, along with passengers, in about 10 minutes as schedules were very tight and the D&K stood to lose 34s to the Post Office for every minute that the mails were late in Dublin. The D&K carried the mails from Kingstown to Dublin (Westland Row) and they were then transferred by road to the General Post Office (scene of the Easter Rising in 1916) in Sackville Street (now O'Connell Street) for onward delivery before breakfast time. In 1855 sorting vehicles were introduced by the Great Southern & Western Railway. These were four-wheeled carriages, 18 ft long with pick-up and set-down apparatus for non-stop transfer of mails. Bogie-type vehicles came into use from 1900. All had apparatus fitted and this system remained in use until 10 June 1969. Coras Iompair Eireann (CIE) inherited a number of these vehicles and only introduced new ones in 1957. These were ten four-wheelers, each 30 ft long and weighing 13½ tons, with no apparatus fitted. In 1958 seven 61 ft 6 in bogie Travelling Post Office vans were built with handling equipment, and a further three similar vehicles were introduced in 1968, rebuilt from passenger coaches.

IRRS/Herbert Richards

On arrival at the new terminal west of Carlisle Pier, Dun Laoghaire, foot passengers from 'Irish Mail' boats travel the 7 miles to Dublin on the DART suburban electric train service to Dublin Connolly station (previously Amiens Street). This rail route has been in existence to Westland Row (now Pearse) since the Dublin & Kingstown Railway started its services on 17 December 1834, predating a similar rail connection on the British mainland, between Liverpool and London, by some four years. When the line was first built it was to the British gauge of 4 ft 8½ in, but on 18 October 1855 this was converted to the Irish standard of 5 ft 3 in.

The Dublin & Kingstown Railway (D&K) was the first railway anywhere in Ireland and received Royal Assent on 6 September 1831, having first failed to secure this in 1825. The estimated cost for construction of the railway was £130,000, and the Board of Public Works was approached for assistance. The BPW thought the project rather expensive and the plans of Alexander Nimmo, who was first engaged to survey the route, were examined by Charles Vignoles who had been appointed Chief Engineer. He re-estimated construction costs at £126,406 and the BPW, after some delay, approved a loan for this sum to the railway company.

William Dargan, who had been supervisor to Thomas Telford on the building of the Holyhead Road, was appointed contractor, with work beginning at Salthill on 11 April 1833. The intention was to open the line in July 1834, but delays with sea embankments meant that the first journey did not take place until 9 October. The line was due to be opened officially two weeks later, but damage to a bridge and flooding led to a two-month delay. The line finally opened at 9 a.m. on 17 December 1834, with the locomotive *Hibernia* hauling the first train from Westland Row to Dunleary, as it was spelt in those days. Although there was no opening ceremony, nearly 5,000 passengers were carried that day and the directors and their friends dined at the Salthill Hotel in celebration.

Two years prior to the opening of the D&K, the English and Irish Post Offices were merged, which offered the potential for through mail services between London and Dublin. With the opening of the D&K, and the possibility of the planned London & Birmingham Railway winning a number of contracts for carriage of mails in mainland Britain, the directors of the L&B sent a representative to report on the new Irish line in 1836. His report to the L&B board, on 21 May 1836, gives an idea of the way the line was run:

The Dublin & Kingstown Railway is 7 miles in length. Trains start every half hour simultaneously from Dublin and from Kingstown, Sundays excepted, when they leave every quarter of an hour. Nothing but passengers and their luggage, and parcels are taken. No other type of traffic is considered. No train stops at more than two stations on the line, each of the five stopping places receiving alternate preference, which diminishes and equalises time of transit. All passengers are charged the same fare and the three classes are distinguished by the colour of the coaches.

Coaches were colour-coded to assist the illiterate. First class were purple, second class were yellow or green and third class were blue, and tickets matched these colours. Trains were usually made up of one first-class carriage, two second class and three third class. At this time fares between Kingstown and Dublin were 1s, 8d and 6d, respectively, per single journey. Even this proved too expensive for men who were employed at Kingstown harbour and lived with their families in Dublin; they usually lodged at Kingstown and just travelled home at weekends.

Following the opening of a rail connection between Euston and Liverpool, mails from these boats was carried by the D&K from 1839. Thus, when the 'Irish Mail' began operating from Euston to Holyhead, mails taken from packet boats operating between Holyhead and Kingstown were automatically carried to Dublin via the D&K, as were mail packet passengers.

Dun Laoghaire, showing the junction from Carlisle Pier, 1970. From its earliest days the pier was served by a railway line which allowed rapid transit of passengers and mails from packet boats. However, the tight curves along the pier could not accommodate modern rolling-stock and the prohibitive costs of altering track levels to that of the main line, after its level had been lowered for clearance purposes following electrification, forced closure on 11 October 1980. Passengers now have to walk to make the connection between pier and main line.

IRRS/Herbert Richards

Dun Laoghaire station with a train about to leave for Dublin, headed by class I3 0–6–2T locomotiv
No. 670, 1954. This locomotive was one of five built by the Great Southern Railways for the Dublin–Bra
services. Four out of five were withdrawn in 1959 and no. 673 in 1962, following the introduction of diese
railcars. The second and third coaches are very interesting: they were built in 1939 as battery electric railcars fo
the Dublin–Bray services. There were four two-car articulated sets, two built in 1932 and a further two in 1939
All four were withdrawn in 1949 when the batteries were due for renewal. The electric equipment was remove
and they ran as ordinary locomotive-hauled coaches for a few more years.

IRRS/L. Hylan

Opposite: General Motors Co-Co No. 081 heading towards Dublin with an express from the south after calling a
Dun Laoghaire, 1977. Before the outbreak of the First World War there were three sailings from Kingstown t
Holyhead a day, two 'Irish Mail' boats and an LNWR steamer. Often two boat trains were provided for each sailin
because so many through carriages were operated by other Irish railway companies offering passengers a direc
service alongside the packet boats. Timings were tight, the second train not due to arrive at Kingstown unti
3 minutes before the boat was due to leave. The night 'Irish Mail' boat arrived in Kingstown at 5.30 a.m. and th
connecting train left at 5.37 a.m. This train was a heavy one, carrying through carriages for Cork and Belfast, a
well as Great Southern & Western Railway and Great Northern Railway breakfast cars which would go throug
on respective mail trains. There were also Midland Great Western Railway coaches for Dublin Broadstone
Passengers on these coaches had to change at Dublin for the 'Limited Mail' to continue their journeys westward.

IRRS/Herbert Richard

A Bo-Bo engine propelling a Dublin-bound train out of Dun Laoghaire station, 1975. CIE, which had taken over the Irish railway system as a private company from 1 January 1945 and became a State-owned operation in 1950, dieselised the Dun Laoghaire–Dublin route in 1955, when 60 1200 hp Co-Co locos for main line use and 34 550 hp Bo-Bo for branch line use were delivered from Metropolitan-Vickers, Manchester. It was the Bo-Bo engines that were used on the Dun Laoghaire line, and they survived on these services until the line was electrified between 1979 and 1984.

IRRS/Herbert Richards

The interior of one of the new electric trains, 1984. Electrification of the suburban line between Howth and Bray, which includes the Dun Laoghaire–Dublin line, has been the only large-scale electrification of the Irish railway system. An overhead catenary system, with a power supply of 1,500 volts DC, was decided upon with a computer system of control, based at Connolly, Dublin. These trains were first delivered in February 1983 and form the DART suburban electric system that foot passengers use from boats at Dun Laoghaire to Dublin. With the British main line between Euston and Crewe and the Irish connection now electrified, if the section between Crewe and Holyhead was also electrified there would be fully electrified trains all the way from Dublin to Paris, via the Channel Tunnel, and beyond.

IRRS/Herbert Richards

A boat train, headed by locomotive No. B201, approaches Lansdowne Road station, home of the Irish Rugby Union team, 1971. Boats used for 'Irish Mail' services also took mail from the USA that had been landed at Queenstown, in the south-west of Ireland, and was carried to Kingstown by rail between 1893 and 1905, saving considerable time on delivery to England. If the arrival of the ship at Queenstown meant that there would not be a connection at Kingstown, then American mails were carried to Dublin (North Wall) where a special boat and train from Holyhead was provided by the LNWR. The Great Southern & Western Railway provided a twice-weekly mail train between Dublin and Cork in connection with the American mails. The Cork–Dublin trains ran non-stop, except for taking on water. On arrival at Dublin the mails were carried forward by the D&K to the packet port. These trains continued running into the 1920s, long after the American mail business had ceased.

IRRS/Herbert Richards

A diesel multiple-unit train at Merrion, between Dublin and Dun Laoghaire, *c.* 1970. The first passenger stock used on the line was provided by several companies. The frames, some of which had bodies fitted, were provided by British businesses. These were 17 ft long, 6 ft 1½ in wide, with a 7 ft wheelbase. Other British-made frames were sent to Ireland to be bodied by the local firms of Dawsons and Courtney & Stephens. First-class compartments held six passengers on cushioned seats, each coach holding a maximum of eighteen people. Second-class coaches had eight to a compartment and carried twenty-four passengers, while in third-class coaches there were five passengers to a seat. Totally open carriages and fourth-class accommodation never existed on the D&K. In the 1880s passenger accommodation improved, with cushioned seats provided in third class, and lavatory facilities fitted in first- and second-class coaches. Over the years passenger rolling-stock improved in parallel with that in Britain.

IRRS/Herbert Richards

A Diesel Multiple Unit is seen on the Dublin–Dun Laoghaire line, 1971. Like Britain, the Irish railway system expanded rapidly in the latter half of the nineteenth century and when the City of Dublin Junction Railway, sponsored by the Great Northern Railway, the Dublin Wicklow & Wexford Railway and the City of Dublin Steam Packet Company, opened in 1891 it improved the transit of mails across Dublin and provided a rail connection between Kingstown Pier and the rest of the Irish system. With the construction of the City of Dublin Junction Railway, Westland Row station ceased to be a terminus and carried through lines served by two platforms, with three-bay platforms for suburban services, including 'mail' trains from Kingstown. All mail traffic has been funnelled through Westland Row from the very earliest days of the 'Irish Mail', but today passengers pass through Westland Row to Connolly, formerly Amiens Street of the Dublin & Drogheda Railway, which is closer to the centre of the capital.

IRRS/Herbert Richards

A 2–4–2 'Mail Tank' approaches Westland Row with a train from Dun Laoghaire, 1949. The first motive power used on the D&K comprised three British-built George Forester and three Sharp Brothers locomotives. These were 2–2–0s with 5 ft drivers and 3 ft 6 in leading wheels. Delays created in the turning of these locos forced the D&K to look at the possibility of locos carrying their own coke and water. When two new engines were ordered the company insisted that Forresters provide locos of this type, thus creating the first tank engines ever to work on a public railway. In 1841 the company was the first to build its own locomotive at its Grand Canal Street works. It was a 2–2–2 tank designed by the company's engineer, Richard Pimm, and was named *Princess* after Queen Victoria's first daughter, born the previous November.

IRRS/J.M. Robbins

Another 2–4–2 'Mail Tank' at Westland Row, Dublin, with its train, 1949. As the terminus for 'Irish Mail' traffic from Euston until 1891, arrival at Westland Row completed a journey covered by millions of letters and passengers.

IRRS/J.M. Robbins

Average Times of Mails, London to Dublin

Date	Time	Land Travel	Sea Travel
1710	7–14 days	Private Coach or Horseback	Sailing Packet
1780	5 days	Stage Coach	Sailing Packet
1812	4 days	Mail Coach	Sailing Packet
1817	55 hrs	Holyhead Mail Coach	Steam Packet (to Howth)
1826	50 hrs	Holyhead Mail Coach	Admiralty Steam Packet (to Kingstown)
1830	35 hrs	New Holyhead Mail Coach	Admiralty Steam Packet (to Kingstown)
1836–8	32 hrs	New Holyhead Mail Coach	Admiralty Steam Packet (to Kingstown)

Coaches ceased in 1839.

Date	Time	Land Travel	Sea Travel
1839	22½ hrs	L&B and GJR	Admiralty Steam Packet from Liverpool
1848	15¾ hrs	LNWR and CHR	Admiralty Steam Packet from Holyhead
1850	14½ hrs	LNWR and CHR	CDSPC
1858	14 hrs	LNWR	CDSPC
1860	11½ hrs	LNWR	CDSPC
1871	11 hrs 10 mins	LNWR	CDSPC
1884	10 hrs 40 mins	LNWR	CDSPC
1885	10 hrs 20 mins	LNWR	CDSPC
1919	10 hrs 10 mins	LNWR	CDSPC
1934	9 hrs 24 mins	LMS	LMS
1939	8 hrs 50 mins	LMS	LMS
1955	8 hrs 30 mins	BR	BR
1975	8 hrs 20 mins	BR	BR
1986	7 hrs 50 mins	BR	Sealink
1990–1	8 hrs	BR	Stena Sealink
1991–6	7 hrs 49 mins	BR	Stena Sealink
1997–	5 hrs 45 mins	Virgin Trains	Stena Lines

ACKNOWLEDGEMENTS

I should like to record my gratitude to all of those people and organisations who have assisted with research and told me anecdotes connected with the story of the 'Irish Mail'. Certainly, the work would have been far more difficult without their help.

Those organisations to whom I am grateful are: Gwynedd Archive Service, Llangefni, Ynys Môn; the Public Record Office, Kew; the National Railway Museum, York; Penmaenmawr Public Library; Stena Lines and B&I Ferries; National Archive of Ireland, Dublin; Coras Iompair Eireann, Ireland; Irish Railway Record Society, Dublin (especially Mr Herbert Richards); and The Post Office, London.

Individual assistance was given by Mr S. Lewis, Peter Owen, Gwyn Roberts, Brenda Roberts, Phillip Vaughan Davies, Joan and Arthur Truby, Maelgwyn Williams, Jim Roberts, Marian and Alvin Forrest, Roger Croston and Colin Marsden.

To all of these people I should like to offer my sincere thanks, and to any others I may have omitted to mention. Finally, I should like to thank Hilary and Gary who have to endure falling over my research material and papers as they go around the house.

BR 9F 2–10–0 No. 92203, now preserved and named *Black Prince*, is departing from Penmaenmawr sidings with a ballast train, late 1950s. To transport stone products from the quarries above Penmaenmawr loading hoppers and railway sidings were provided behind the station. The ballast from Penmaenmawr is still used under the railway tracks that carry the 'Irish Mail'.

Gwyn Roberts